Turkish
Miniature
Paintings
&
Manuscripts

from the collection of
Edwin Binney, 3rd

Turkish Miniature Paintings and Manuscripts

Turkish Miniature Paintings and Manuscripts / FROM THE COLLECTION OF EDWIN BINNEY, 3rd

by *Edwin Binney, 3rd*

THE METROPOLITAN MUSEUM OF ART
LOS ANGELES COUNTY MUSEUM OF ART

All photographs, including that for the cover, by the Photo Studio, Metropolitan Museum, except for Cat. Nos. 1, 10 (*shamseh* page and fols. 27v, 70r, 193v), 14, 17, 19, 28, 31, and 35; design by Peter Oldenburg; composition by Finn Typographic Service; printing by the Meriden Gravure Company

LIBRARY OF CONGRESS CATALOGING IN PUBLICATION DATA

Binney, Edwin.
  Turkish miniature paintings and manuscripts from the collection of Edwin Binney, 3rd.

  Catalog of an exhibition held in the Metropolitan Museum of Art, New York and the Los Angeles County Museum of Art.
  Bibliography: p.
  1. Illumination of books and manuscripts, Turkish—Exhibitions. 2. Miniature painting, Turkish—Exhibitions. 3. Binney, Edwin—Art collections. I. New York (City). Metropolitan Museum of Art. II. Los Angeles Co., Calif. Museum of Art, Los Angeles. III. Title.

ND3211.B56   745.6'7'09561   73-11016

ISBN 0-87099-077-2

Contents

Foreword

Examples of the Turkish pictorial arts outside the Topkapu Saray Library in Istanbul are rare—a well-known fact that Dr. Binney demonstrates again in his introduction to this catalogue. Why so rare? For one thing, this art never achieved widespread support or appreciation within the Turkish empire. It was fostered only by the sultan's court and kept within the confines of the royal establishments. The fact that the Turks were Sunnis who followed the canonical law more strictly than, for instance, the Iranians may have a good deal to do with the limited number of existing works illustrated by Turkish miniature painters.

The major museums and libraries of the world possess relatively few examples of Turkish miniature paintings and manuscripts. In the private sector, only two enthusiastic connoisseurs have acquired large and representative collections: the late Sir Chester Beatty, founder of the Chester Beatty Library in Dublin, and the author of this catalogue, a loyal friend of the Islamic Department of The Metropolitan Museum of Art. Aided by his connoisseurship and wide knowledge of the arts of the Near and Middle East, Dr. Binney has been able by painstaking and well-informed endeavors to collect every form of Turkish painting. His collection ranges from a rare example of the late fifteenth century through the more numerous paintings of the nineteenth century, when the art was increasingly influenced by European styles. The collection contains historical accounts of the lives and accomplishments of earlier sultans as well as illuminated works dealing with saints or legendary heroes. There are portraits of sultans and of handsome youths and maidens, renditions of historic buildings, decorative illuminations, and various forms of the art of calligraphy.

While Turkish painting was contemporary with that of Iran and Mughal India, in nearly all ways it was distinguishable, not only in its different forms of dress and headgear and the more formal presentation of the figures, but also in its more simplified and at times monumentalized forms of trees, landscapes, and architecture. At the same time the Turkish artist had a keen eye for details, an attitude that led in the course of time to realistic portrayals of figures and scenes. Such close observation eventually made the artists turn to exaggeration—even caricature. All of this helped to make Turkish painting something unique, even though its heritage from Persian painting and its European influences are easily recognized.

Dr. Binney's well-illustrated catalogue offers the general public and the student alike an excellent survey of Turkish painting and an insight into the special qualities of this diverse art. His collection, so generously lent to us, represents a cultural achievement worthy of honoring the Republic of Turkey on the occasion of its fiftieth anniversary.

RICHARD ETTINGHAUSEN
Consultative Chairman,
Department of Islamic Art

Preface

"The materials available [to trace the history of Turkish painting] are too fragmentary, and are likely to remain so till the whole extent of the contents of Turkish libraries is revealed. Turkish fine manuscripts and miniatures elsewhere are not very numerous." (J. V. S. Wilkinson, introduction to Minorsky, *The Chester Beatty Library, a Catalogue of the Turkish Manuscripts and Miniatures*, 1958)

"One of the major reasons [for the neglect of Turkish pictorial art] is the fact that there was, and still is, very little first-rate or well documented material in European museums and libraries, and probably even less in those of the United States. The vast majority of it has remained in Turkey where it was at first almost inaccessible." (Richard Ettinghausen, introduction to *Turkey, Ancient Miniatures*, 1961)

"Firstly, the greater part of the rich collection in the Istanbul libraries has been inadequately described in the past.... The second difficulty is far more serious—the scarcity of material outside Turkey...." (G. M. Meredith-Owens, *Turkish Miniatures*, 1963)

"Of all the schools of painting from Islamic countries those of Turkey are most rarely represented in Western collections since the vast majority of the original output has been kept in Istanbul, particularly in the library of the Topkapu Palace Museum." (Richard Ettinghausen, in *Islamic Art from the Collection of Edwin Binney 3rd*, 1966)

"[Turkish painting] is still unfamiliar outside Turkey, as almost nothing about it has been published in the West, and very few paintings have ever reached Western collections." (Ernst J. Grube, in *Metropolitan Museum of Art Bulletin*, January 1968)

Each of the scholars quoted here alludes to the treasures of Ottoman miniature painting to be found almost nowhere but in the country of their origin, specifically, in the Topkapu Saray and other museum-libraries of Istanbul. Since these Turkish libraries are only now beginning to catalogue and reproduce their paintings, the question remains: Where, outside Istanbul, is it possible to study Ottoman miniatures in any depth? Three national libraries in Europe have reasonably extensive collections: those in Vienna, Paris, and London. All three are important for reasons other than aesthetic. Vienna saw its first Turkish manuscripts in the sixteenth century as part of the booty of war. In the 1660s, Louis XIV's finance minister, Colbert, instructed French agents in the Near East to send home foreign texts—texts that found their way into the royal (later national) library. The English, with tremendous interests in India at the same time, were avid collectors of manuscripts from Turkey as well as other countries in the Near and Far East. In 1888, when Charles Rieu published his *Catalogue of the Turkish Manuscripts in the British Museum*, he listed 483 items, yet only twelve of these contained miniatures. From the beginnings summarized here come most of the examples of Turkish painting outside Istanbul. (Of the three national libraries, only the British Museum has systematically continued to add to its Turkish collection.)

One private collection deserves to rank with the national libraries. The late Chester Beatty, whose extensive holdings of Persian, Indian, and Turkish manuscripts and miniatures make Dublin a necessary stopping place for the historian of Islamic art, amassed ninety-three Turkish manuscripts and albums. Of these, thirty-three contain miniatures or diagrams. The excellent catalogue of this collection, published in 1958 by Professor Minorsky, with its valuable reproductions, has done more to shed light on the body of Turkish paintings outside the Istanbul libraries than any previous volume.

In the United States the search for Ottoman miniatures is even more difficult than in western Europe. A few important single paintings are in the Museum of Fine Arts, Boston, and the Freer Gallery, Washington, D.C. Others are in the Pierpont Morgan Library, New York, the Cleveland Museum of Art, and a few private collections, while single miniatures exist in Worcester and Providence. The Metropolitan Museum of Art has a collection, rather than a few separate items, largely by default. When that Museum sought to highlight its Turkish holdings in all media in its *Bulletin* of January 1968, only eight leaves with miniatures could be reproduced with the ceramics, metalworks, rugs, and textiles.

This catalogue presents a collection of Ottoman manuscripts and miniatures. I have no illusion that each of the pictures can match in aesthetic merit those in New York or Boston. On the other hand, this is probably the largest and the most well-rounded group in existence outside of Istanbul, London, Paris, Vienna, and Dublin. With this thought in mind, I wish to dedicate the catalogue to:

Those whose previous works have helped me to understand and love Ottoman miniature painting, and those who may possibly use and value this token of my collecting mania.

Three scholars (as well as some others whose names are listed in the Bibliography) have assisted me personally in the preparation of this catalogue: Richard Ettinghausen of the Metropolitan Museum of Art, the dean of international Islamicists, G. M. Meredith-Owens of the University of Toronto, and Walter B. Denny of the University of Massachusetts. Without their continued kindness in the sharing of their specialized but vast knowledge, the complex problems of attribution and dating could not have been resolved as fully as they are herein. My thanks are also extended to Suzan Akkan of the Library of the University of California, Los Angeles, who helped with preliminary translations, and to Marie Lukens Swietochowski of the Metropolitan Museum for her careful reading of the proofs and her meticulous scholarship.

And here I offer a note on the transliteration of Turkish. One of the changes brought about by Atatürk, founder of the Republic of Turkey, was the abandonment of the Arabic alphabet in favor of the European. The complex richness of Turkish vowel sounds, for which written Arabic had no equivalent, greatly hampered an accurate transcription of the language. Only in recent times, by the use of numerous diacritical marks, can modern Turkish be properly written. The proliferation of various accents, however, presents difficulties for the Western reader. Accordingly, it has seemed wise in this catalogue to simplify many of the proper and specialized names: for example, *nakkash-hane* rather than *nakkaşhane*; *Gench Osman* rather than *Genç Osman*; *Vali Jan* rather than *Velican*; and the very recognizable *Sulayman* the Magnificent instead of *Süleyman*. One Turkish letter can only be approximated. The undotted *i*, used for the common unvoiced vowel sound, provides too great a challenge to typesetters and proofreaders of English. In its place I use an unaccented *u*, as in *Topkapu*, rather than a dotted *i*, as did the makers of the delightful movie *Topkapi*, about a daring robbery in the old sultans' palace.

E. B., 3rd

Introduction

Even before the advent of Islam, Turkish nomadic tribes ranging between the Caspian Sea and Lake Baikal (the present Soviet Central Asia) were known to their more cultivated neighbors, the Chinese to the east and the Sasanians in Persia to the south. Many in the western group of these nomads were converted by the proselytizing force of the Islamic religion and turned their attention toward the Muslim world. By the ninth century, Turks were holding important positions throughout the Near East, and one dynasty, the Tulunids, ruled Egypt in semi-autonomy under the weak suzerainty of the caliph of Baghdad. The military strength of Mahmud of Ghazna, a Turkish leader who carved out his own principality, carried Islam permanently from what is now Afghanistan into North India at the end of the tenth century. Other Turks, the Seljuks, controlled the whole of the caliphate after 1038, except Egypt and North Africa, and, as the ruling family split into separate branches, reigned over many smaller domains in the Near East. The Seljuks in Persia were succeeded by the Mongols, and they in turn, in the fourteenth century, by the descendants of Timur, another Turkish conqueror. Former Turkish slaves in Egypt, the Mamluks, controlled that country from 1250 to 1517, and a later branch of the Timurids ruled India as the Mughal emperors until 1857. Politically, then, Islam has owed much to the Turks.

Most of the rulers of these Turkish dynasties patronized painters, as, of course, did their non-Turkish allies and rivals. It does seem awkward, however (despite the insistence of modern Turkish art historians) to remove from the geographic unity of Persian, Indian, or Mamluk painting those parts for which Turks were patrons in order to create a pan-Turkish school. Instead, let us concentrate on the painting produced for one particular dynasty of rulers that rose and fell in the country that still bears the name of its larger racial family—Turkey.

Near the end of the thirteenth century and the beginning of the fourteenth, there appeared in the troubled territorial politics of the Anatolian peninsula a force of new Turks, under the leadership of a warlord named Osman, or Othman. The decline of the more centralized authority of the Seljuks of Rum, as Anatolia was then called, and petty wars among the Christian principalities that dated from the time of the fourth Crusade made the moment ripe for the rise of a vital new dynasty. By the time of the death of Osman I in 1326 and the succession of his son Orkhan, these tribesmen, who were called Osmanli (or Ottoman by Westerners), had seized a small enclave of former Christian territory to the south and east of the Sea of Marmara. From these modest beginnings a series of warlike sons succeeded their warlike fathers and boasted that no leader bequeathed his sultanate in the same size as he had received it—always larger. Major achievements were the capture of the former Christian city of Nicaea, the overthrow of several of the many autonomous Turkish chieftains to the south and east, and the establishment of a foothold on the peninsula of Gallipoli, on the European side of the Dardanelles. The Byzantine Empire seemed doomed until the armies of Timur, which had ravaged Persia, Mesopotamia, and Syria, defeated and captured Sultan Bayazid I at the Battle of Ankara (1402). This setback for Ottoman arms granted a respite of a half century for the dying Byzantine state. The rapid reconsolidation of Osmanli supremacy over the territories stripped from the sultanate by Timur went on in the interim.

Under Mehmet II (known as Mehmet *Fatih*, "the Conqueror," reigned 1452–1480), whose first wish at his accession was the conquest of the Byzantine capital, the Ottomans succeeded in ending the rule of the more than eleven-centuries-old empire, and made Constantinople their new capital (1453) in place of Adrianople (Edirne) in Thrace. With Mehmet *Fatih* begins the known history of Ottoman painting. Heretofore, the rulers had been concerned chiefly with war, but the new capital seemed to add another psychological facet to the sultan's character. The ruler of the world's most honored city needed to be more than a successful warrior. He must also be a Maecenas. Mehmet II, a poet himself, protected scholars, writers, and artists of all kinds. Visits by Costanzo da Ferrara and Gentile Bellini to Constantinople at the particular request of the sultan to the King of Naples and the Doge of Venice show an enlightened attitude toward painting.[1] The productions of these and other Italian artists may be said to inaugurate the Ottoman school of painting, but they certainly did not greatly influence it.

The development of the sultans as art patrons, however, in no way detracted from the success of their armies. If few works date from the reign of "the Conqueror,"[2] the rule of his son Bayazid II (1481–1512) saw the production of a group of manuscripts (see Cat. No. 1). The short reign of Selim I *Yavuz* ("the Grim"; 1512–1520) was little more than a series of wars—in Europe, Persia, and Egypt. The occupation of the Iranian capital Tabriz in 1514, upon successful completion of the war against Shah Ismail the Safavid, was crucial for the future of Ottoman art. Seven hundred families of artists were brought back to Constantinople after the campaigns. A similar mass migration occurred after the conquest of Egypt in 1517. There, Selim ended the rule of the Mamluk Turks and assumed the title of caliph when the last of the later Abbasids, who had been pensioners of the Mamluks, was deposed. Thereafter the sultans were not only territorial princes, they were religious heads of Islam, at least for the orthodox Muslims. The Mamluk domains that were now added to the burgeoning Ottoman Empire included Syria, Palestine, and Arabia, as well as Egypt. From each of these newly conquered territories, the best artists of every kind were sent to Istanbul to practice their crafts and teach native Turks to master them also.

Selim's son Sulayman *Kanuni* ("the Lawgiver" to the Turks, but called "the Magnificent" in Europe; 1520–1566) dominated the whole of eastern Europe and the Near East as did his contemporary, Emperor Charles V in the West. Serbia was overrun and Belgrade captured (1521), the Knights of St. John of Jerusalem were defeated and forced to evacuate their citadel on the island of Rhodes, and, in 1526, Hungary was overrun and her king killed at the Battle of Mohács. Three years later Vienna was besieged, although unsuccessfully. Persia was again invaded and Tabriz captured several times. The Magnificent Sultan was still the greatest territorial prince in the world! The ateliers of his painters strove to produce works worthy of his position, and his head scribes produced the *tughra*, or legal monogram (Cat. No. 3) that introduced his imperial *firmans*, or decrees.

It is exactly from the reign of Sulayman that we begin to have some knowledge of the *nakkash-hane*, or court ateliers. Part of a register was recently found by Oktay Aslanapa in the Topkapu Museum. In it are listed sixteen painters, including three portraitists (*musavvir*), and thirteen specialists in mural decorations and flowers (*nakkash*). Dr. Aslanapa is certain that these figures reflect the presence of artists brought from Tabriz in 1514. Later in the century the historian Mustafa Ali wrote a didactic account of Turkish painters and calligraphers, the *Menaqib-i Hünerveran* (1587), in which he mentioned the artists of his time. Supplementing these two records, we have registers of the artists' guild, particularly those of 1525/1526 and 1557/1558. From these sources we find that the imperial studio included, in addition to Turkish painters, Hungarians, Albanians, Circassians, and Moldavians, as well as the expected Persians with their Turkish-born sons. It is obvious that Persian influence was paramount. Persian had always been the language and literature of culture in the non-Arab Muslim, and Persian painting, particularly that from the courts of the Timurid princes, ranked supreme. The Treasury in the Topkapu Palace already contained important Persian manuscripts seized during campaigns in Iran. Yet it was exactly at the time of the strongest Persian influence that Ottoman Turkish painting began to find a style of its own and to experiment in fields far from the Persian models.

The explanation is twofold. Persian miniature painting was firmly wedded to Persian literature. The national epic, the *Shah Nameh* of Firdousi, together with the *Khamseh* (quintet of tales) by Nizami, the poetical romances of Jami, the *Bustan* and *Gulistan* of Sa'di, and the *Divan* of Hafiz were the works most often illustrated by Persian painters. The characters portrayed might be clad in contemporary fashion, and the principals might, as a delicate compliment to a reigning prince, resemble living people, but all were essentially figures of fantasy. Even if the stories concerned semi-historical personages, the people illustrated were of legendary grandeur: the hero Rustam, the handsome Khosrau who loved the fair Shirin, or Majnun who died of love for Layla, like Romeo for Juliet. Even when the Persians made a formal portrait of a king or courtier, it was most often an idealized likeness.

Certainly, Turkish artists illustrated the Persian texts, both in the original Persian (Cat. No. 1) and in Turkish adaptations (Cat. No. 17), and therefore retained affinities with Persian pictorial usage. But literary genres almost completely absent from Persian tradition were espoused during the reign of Sulayman the Magnificent and were continued thereafter.

The illustrating of a history of the reigning sultan, or a posthumous tribute to his rule, became the most important non-Persian kind of painting in Turkey. It was a sort of "public relations" effort, a monumental presentation of the world conquerors, of the physical grandeur of their persons and courts, and of the invincibility of their huge armies. These large works and the individual portraits (Cat. Nos. 8, 19, 23) and illustrated genealogies that appeared for the same purpose do not portray people seen through a rosy-hued lens as in Persia. They are valid social documents, with a powerful tendency toward realism. This series of works begins with a *Selim Nameh*[3] prepared early in the reign of Sulayman as a tribute to his father. There follows a *Sulayman Nameh* for "the Magnificent" himself in 1558.[4] During the reign of Selim II "the Sot" (1566–1574), who gave a Koran (Cat. No. 7) to the mosque he founded in Edirne and whose portraits are in this collection (Cat. Nos. 8, 23), a *History of the Siege of* [the Hungarian city of] *Szigeth*[5] was also completed. The major painter of his court, the retired admiral-director of the imperial shipyards, Haydar Reis, called Nigari (1484–1574), may be the artist who copied the portraits after Clouet and Cranach (Cat. Nos. 6a, b). Nigari died in the same year as his patron. Under Selim's son and successor, Murad III (1574–1595), Ottoman miniature painting reached its apogee.

Historical works continued to be written and illustrated for the new sultan: histories of his father (the *Shah Nameh-e Selim Khan* by the historiographer Loqman[6]), of his grandfather (the *Tabaqat al-mamalik* in Vienna[7] and the biography by the same Loqman in the Beatty Library, Dublin[8]), as well as of himself (Loqman's *Shahinshah Nameh* in two volumes dated 1581 and 1592, in the University Library, Istanbul[9]).

Histories of individual military campaigns: in Georgia in 1578–1579 (two in the British Museum[10] and one in the Topkapu Saray[11]); in Persia from 1578 to 1583 (University Library[12]); in Genjeh in 1588[13]; and previously in Arabia and Tunisia under Sinan Pasha (University Library[14]) were also produced for the same imperial patron. Chief of these works, also linked to Murad III, was the *Hüner Nameh*, again by Loqman, in two volumes dated 1584 and 1589, the first containing forty-five miniatures, the second, sixty-five, in the Topkapu Saray.[15] (The second volume, treating the reign of Sulayman I, was exhibited in the United States from 1966 to 1968. No. 11 in this catalogue is related to these illustrations.)

The *Sur Nameh,* or *Festival Book,* commemorating the celebrations for the circumcision of Murad's son, the future Mehmet III, containing 437 illustrations (in the Topkapu Saray)[16] was considered too valuable to send to America. These historical works were only part of the output of the imperial ateliers.

Ottoman illustrated religious texts may have been produced even earlier than the first historical works. (The early *Sulayman Nameh* of the Beatty collection, which can be dated about 1500, concerns the Biblical Solomon rather than his Turkish namesake.) Copies of similar texts by Fuzuli, Lami'i Chelebi, and the ubiquitous Loqman appeared commonly during the reign of Murad III also, but a religious manuscript such as Cat. No. 4 is uncommon in the first half of the sixteenth century. The religious texts of the latter part of the century are as lavish as the historical works and just as typically Turkish, rather than Persian. Iranian literature had few illustrated texts on religious subjects,[17] and in this area the Turks experimented rather than copied. (For leaves from similar religious works, see Cat. Nos. 12, 13, 18a, b.)

Elegant line drawings, often heightened with gold and colors, were also common during the reign of the royal connoisseur. A group of marvelous dragons fighting other mythological beasts or lurking in fabulous vegetation (Cat. No. 5) come from the previous reign, but continued to be made under Murad III. These dragons reflect a Chinese influence comparable to the known imperial predilection for blue-and-white porcelain ware of the Ming dynasty. Another foreign influence, this time from Transoxiana, is shown in a series of Oriental princesses, or houris of the Islamic paradise, several of them inscribed with the name of the Ottoman painter Vali Jan, a pupil of Siyavush the Georgian (Cat. No. 14).[18] Other similar drawings show Mongol or Uzbek prisoners (Cat. No. 15). Another unusual genre, typically Turkish rather than Persian, was the use of marbled paper on which

layers of different colors were manipulated to produce extremely complicated patterns (the boards of Cat. No. 2 and the border of Cat. No. 35 are good examples). The most typical product of the ateliers of Murad III in the present exhibition is Cat. No. 10, an extremely rare manuscript with many kinds of miniatures, including two portraits of the sultan himself.

The death of the greatest of the royal patrons did not curtail the production of important books and pictures. During the reigns of his immediate successors Mehmet III (1595–1603), Ahmed I (1603–1617), Mustafa I (1617–1618 and 1622–1623), and Osman II (1618–1622), literary, historical, and religious manuscripts continued to be made for the sultans. Of the last-named genre, the *Fal Nameh (Book of Divination)* by Kalender Pasha[19] was prepared for presentation to Ahmed I (Cat. No. 47 may be from a similar work, or from a Persian adaptation of it). Courtiers and private citizens also commissioned works, of which a small manuscript in this exhibition (Cat. No. 20) is typical. The non-imperial manuscripts have a charm and simplicity that distinguishes them from the more complicated royal works, whether translations from Persian romances (Cat. No. 25) or historical writings (Cat. Nos. 21, 27; the latter is from a manuscript probably prepared for Sultan Osman II). Other non-royal collectors no doubt desired the small and simple series of sultans' portraits (Cat. No. 19) in contrast to the imperial ones (Cat. Nos. 23, 26).

A final genre of painting typical of the Turkish tradition and scarcely seen in the Persian is the exact delineation of buildings and places. This architectural and cartographic interest began early and continued until the end of the Ottoman Empire. As early as 1513 the Turkish mapmaker-sailor Piri Reis pictured America on the western edge of the Atlantic Ocean (map is in the Topkapu Saray). This was not an isolated example. Scarcely twenty years later, the court geographer and historian Matrakji described in the *Menazil Nameh (Itinerary)* by means of text and geographical designs the invasion routes of Sulayman "the Magnificent" in his first expedition against Persia (1534–1536).

From this kind of view of the world, it was a short step to miniatures showing the important buildings of the sultanate. The holy sites of Islam, the Ka'ba at Mecca (Cat. Nos. 10, fol. 27v; 40, fol. 80v; 49, fol. 18v) and the tomb of the Prophet at Medina (Cat. Nos. 40, fol. 81r; 49, fol. 39r), as well as the mosques of the capital and other major cities, provided subjects for Turkish painters in a way they never did for their Iranian contemporaries. Even in a narrative picture such as Cat. No. 31, the architecture of the cities in the background receives greater attention than the episode taking place in front.

The decline in artistry in the seventeenth century is not immediately apparent. One evidence of it is a general coarsening and increase in size of the figures, with an emphasis on the head, which is often too large for the body (Cat. Nos. 9a and 13 show an early instance of this tendency). Another is an accent on caricature, never far removed from Turkish folk art. The begging dervish of Cat. No. 30 and the torlaqs, or wild youths, of Cat. No. 36 are excellent examples.

The later sultans became more and more indolent and pleasure-loving. Fewer of them campaigned actively with their troops. Uprisings in the conquered provinces depleted the energies of the armies and consumed much of the revenue without gaining lands or prestige. The historical works that eulogized the expanding state and its monarchs were abandoned. Individual genre scenes (Cat. Nos. 31, 32) or portraits of harem beauties and flowers satisfied the many aesthetes among the later rulers. Another great Sur Nameh, or Festival Book (like that of Murad III mentioned above), was prepared by the poet Vehbi to commemorate the circumcision of four of the sons of Ahmed III in 1720.[20] This manuscript was exhibited in the United States in 1966–1968. Its 138 miniatures, many of which use the same architectural background to record the processions of the different guilds

before the sultan in the Hippodrome, are a tour de force of the court painter Levni. He and his slightly younger contemporary Abdullah Bukhari (see Cat. No. 35) were the last great painters of the Ottoman tradition. But royal decrees with the distinctive tughra showing the sultan's monogram were still necessary (Cat. No. 37), and courtiers or rich townsmen had its distinctive flourish copied as decorations (Cat. No. 39). Series of royal portraits were also produced (Cat. No. 44), as they had been for earlier reigns. Manuscripts of guidebooks were still prepared for travelers to the holy places of Islam (Cat. Nos. 40, 49); Korans were written for the devout (Cat. No. 41); and pictures were painted for travelers from the West (Cat. Nos. 34a, b; 43 a-d). But with the increasing desire to ape European fashion and art (Cat. Nos. 38a, b), Turkish painting sank as low as the political state, which from the "Sublime Porte" had become by the nineteenth century the "Sick Man of Europe."

One supreme legacy remained from the sultans. At the end of the First World War the Ottomans, like so many of the royal dynasties of Europe, were deposed as political rulers, their empire becoming the Republic of Turkey under Kemal Atatürk, with its capital at Ankara rather than Istanbul. For a time, the cousin of the last sultan took office as caliph, but he was deposed in 1924. Owing to the peaceful way in which the deposition was carried out, the sultans' palaces were not looted, and no frenzied mobs scattered their treasures. By the time of the Ottomans' ultimate exclusion from their country, their presence had saved as a national heritage the bulk of their fabulous collections. The new republic, without the interim of pillage that has destroyed or dispersed so many treasuries of the past, was strong enough to guard its still undreamed-of riches. This is the reason for the supremacy of the Istanbul libraries in the field of Ottoman painting: most of it—and the major percentage of its greatest works—remains where it has always been, on the banks of the Bosphorus and the Golden Horn.

15

NOTES

1. As orthodox Sunnites, the Ottomans would be expected to interpret religious strictures against figural representation in a narrow way. They did not! They did, however, keep their collections of illustrated manuscripts and miniatures in the Seraglio, away from profane, unenlightened eyes.
2. Meredith-Owens (1963, p. 31) gives the titles of the few illustrated manuscripts that date from the reign of Mehmet *Fatih*.
3. Topkapu Saray, Hazine 1597–1598; Stchoukine, I, 1966, Ms. 8.
4. Hazine 1517; Stchoukine, Ms. 21.
5. Hazine 1339; Stchoukine, Ms. 29.
6. A. 3595; Stchoukine, Ms. 30.
7. Stchoukine, Ms. 32.
8. Stchoukine, Ms. 33.
9. Stchoukine, Mss. 32, 53.
10. Stchoukine, Mss. 36, 38.
11. Hazine 1365; Stchoukine, Ms. 44.
12. Yildîz, 2385/105; Stchoukine, Ms. 48.
13. K. 1296; Stchoukine, Ms. 51.
14. Stchoukine, Ms. 54.
15. Hazine 1523, 1524; Stchoukine, Ms. 45.
16. Hazine 1344; Stchoukine, Ms. 39.
17. The *Mi'raj Nameh* dated 1436 (Bibliothèque Nationale) is exceptional, and it is written in Chagatai Turkish, with Uighur script, rather than in Persian. The Turkman *Khavaran Nameh* by ibn Husan of about 1480 (see Grube, *Muslim Miniature Paintings*, 1962, nos. 46–49) was a sort of pastiche of Firdousi's *Shah Nameh*, and its illustrations, although of religious subjects, do not substantially depart from the mainstream of Iranian miniatures.
18. Presumed Uighur influence from a similar Central Asian region may account for the curious series of nomads and demons in the album called "of the Conqueror" (Topkapu Saray, Hazine 2153).
19. Topkapu Saray, Hazine 1703; Stchoukine, Ms. 89.
20. Topkapu Saray, Hazine 3593; Stchoukine, Mss. 88–103.

Turkish Miniature Paintings and Manuscripts

1

Manuscript of the Mantiq al-Tayr by Attar.

In Persian. 171 ff. with 3 miniatures in the Turkish style of ca. 1480–1490, *unwan* (double frontispiece). Simple leather binding, ca. 1550–1560. Size (binding): 6¾ x 4½ x ⅞ in. A former owner has added the date 1150/1737 beneath the otherwise undated colophon, but this addition has nothing to do with the text.

The simplicity and small size of this manuscript mask its huge importance. It is one of fewer than ten known manuscripts illustrated with Turkish miniatures that can be dated before about 1500. The Bibliothèque Nationale, Paris, possesses the earliest: an *Iskandar Nameh* by Ahmedi dated 1416 (Stchoukine, I, 1966, Ms. 1, pls. I, II). Its illustrations look like typical "Arab miniatures," and only its Turkish text and colophon stating that it was finished at Amasya show that it is the earliest dated Ottoman Turkish illustrated manuscript. (Its miniatures are, however, somewhat later than the date of the colophon.)

The other early texts with pictures date from the reign of Sultan Bayazid II (1481-1512). There are a *Kalila wa Dimna* dated 1495 in Bombay (Stchoukine, I, 1966, Ms. 2, pl. III); a *Khamseh* by Amir Khusrau Dihlavi dated 1498 in the Topkapu Saray (Hazine 799; Stchoukine, Ms. 3, pl. IV); and a *Khusrau o Shirin* dated 1499 in the University Library, Uppsala, Sweden (Stchoukine, Ms. 4). Stylistic similarities to the miniatures in these dated volumes allow attribution to the same period of the undated *Sulayman Nameh* by Sharaf al-din Musa of Bursa, surnamed 'Firdousi the Long," in the Beatty Library, Dublin (Stchoukine, Ms. 5), and the present volume. A Hatifi manuscript of 1498–1499, formerly in the Sir Thomas Phillipps collection, now in the Metropolitan Museum (acc. no. 69.27), and an *Iskandar Nameh* by Ahmedi, dated 1500–1501, in the Topkapu (Hazine 679) complete this group of early manuscripts. An unpublished manuscript in the Fogg Art Museum and a separate miniature showing Majnun disguised before Layla, in the Kraus collection, are mentioned by Grube (1972, pp. 207–208).

The miniatures in the present manuscript bear strong affinities to the simple pictures by Shirazi artists at the courts of the Black and White Sheep Turkmen in the second half of the fifteenth century in Iran. But there are already immediately

شاه... او گفت ای درویش من   چه نیست کار تو پیش در پیش میدانی نه کار گر مبا
خویشتن را اعجبی ره سپار   پیر زد دل امید روبا کشی روز و شب درشت شم عاشق
خامه نه شم نزدم نان غمی   می شنوای گرم لانی د سفته   شهر یارکس گفت او پر رشد
نخ زکن تا رز جسم بیند کین ت   کنت این شب زیده نار آتش   کرون وی نشان و

recognizable Turkish elements. A Persian artist would probably not have painted the flat gold on the wall of the interior scene, fol. 50v, nor the absolutely similar gold sky of fol. 62v. The cypress trees standing in orderly rows against the horizon of fol. 95r and in the upper right of fol. 62v are also common in Turkish painting. The oversimplification in the placing of figures in a landscape was also common in Shiraz at the time, but not to the extent visible here.

The fact that the text is in Persian rather than Turkish in no way detracts from the Turkish attribution. Many sultans and their courtiers were fluent in Persian, the elegant language of Islam (including Turkey and Mughal India), particularly for the writing of poetry.

The subjects of the miniatures are:

fol. 50v: Shaykh San'an explains to his non-Muslim sweetheart that he has given up his religion for her. A mullah asks her what she has done to achieve this. (Cf. Robinson, 1958, no. 502, fol. 45a, illustrating a more complete copy of the *Mantiq al-Tayr* in the Bodleian Library [Ms. Elliott 246].)

fol. 62v: The king and the thorn-gatherer (Robinson, 1958, no. 504, fol. 52b).

fol. 95r: The old woman purchases Yusuf (the Biblical Joseph) at the slave market in Cairo (Robinson, 1958, no. 505, fol. 96a).

fol. 50v   fol. 95r

2

Manuscript in masnavi verse in praise of Sulayman I.

8 ff. and endpapers. Dated: Dhu'l-Hijja, 932/1526, at Samandireh (Byzantine Samandria; Smeredevo, in Serbia). Binding: boards covered with marbled paper, probably contemporary. Endpapers more modern. Size (binding): 10¾ x 7½ x ¼ in.

fol. 1r

This unpretentious little collection of poems for Sulayman the Magnificent (1520–1566) allows a glance at the practices of Ottoman book production early in the reign of the greatest of the sultans. The boards (cardboard rather than leather binding) are covered with marbled paper, a Turkish specialty. The recto of the first folio reveals a calligraphic flourish similar to that of the later, more elaborate *tughras* (Cat. Nos. 3, 37). It shows the word *huwa* (standing for the word "He," as the synonym for God, which is shouted by dervishes for talismanic effect). Surrounding the letter are attributes for the divinity ("He is the great; He is the good; O Lord my God. . . ." etc.).

The headings of the opening pages (exhibited) show parts of *Surah* 61 of the Koran (*As-Saff*, or "The Ranks"). The vertical panels of calligraphy are from verse 13: (left) "Help from God and a nigh victory"; (right) "Give thou good tidings to the Believers [O Muhammed]." It is fitting that the poem is prefaced by this scriptural benediction, for at the time when this text was being prepared Sulayman was starting his campaign against the Hungarians (which resulted in the tremendous victory of Mohács and the death of King Louis II in 1526, followed by the siege of Vienna three years later).

The writing is a simple, stately *nashki*, a style of Islamic calligraphy largely superseded at this time, particularly in Iran, in favor of the more cursive *nastaliq*. The upside-down trefoil of the colophon on fol. 8r is typically Ottoman in its decoration, resembling the complexity of the much later calligraphic ewer of Cat. No. 42.

3

Tughra of Sulayman I.

Ca. 1550–1565. Size: 13⅝ x 16⅛ in.

EX COLL.: Jean Pozzi, Paris.

REPRODUCTIONS FOR COMPARISON: *Art Treasures of Turkey*, 1966, no. 186; *Metropolitan Museum of Art Bulletin*, January 1968, no. 36 and cover; *Skira*, 1966, p. 216; all *tughras* of Sulayman I.

The *tughra*, or ornamental, stylized monogram of the reigning sultan, is not unique to Turkish art, but the swagger and ebullience shown by the Ottoman scribes is completely un-Persian. Whereas European rulers used a seal to legalize their edicts and had a Lord Keeper of the Great (or Privy) Seal, in Constantinople the head scribe of the royal library alone was able to duplicate the complex arabesques of the legalizing *tughra*. One of the glories of the Topkapu Palace Museum is its collections of such "seals," including several examples like this one.

For literature on *tughras*, see Bibliography entries Bombaci, Kühnel, McAllister, Pinder-Wilson, and Wittek.

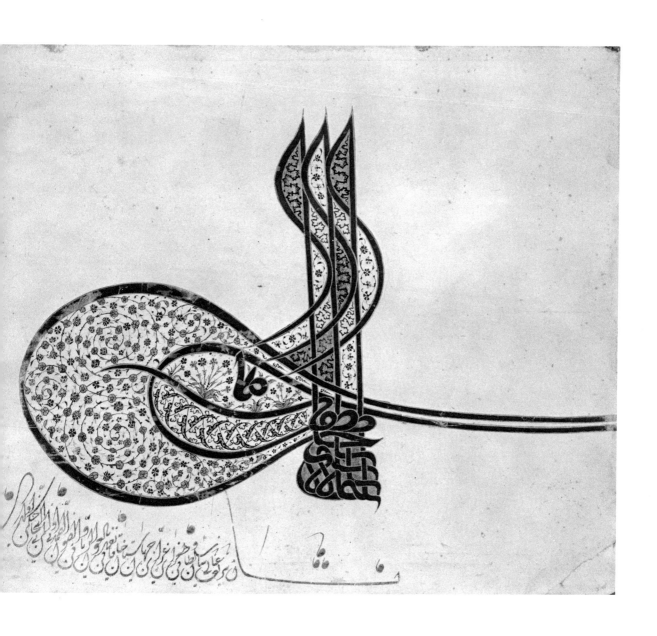

4

Manuscript of the Hadikat al-Su'ada (A History of the Martyrs of the Prophet's Family) by Fuzuli.

In Turkish. 167 ff., 4 miniatures. Ca. 1550. Size (binding): 7⁹⁄₁₆ x 5 x 1⅛ in.

REPRODUCTIONS FOR COMPARISON:
Stchoukine, I, 1966, pl. IX.

The miniatures in this curious manuscript present an uncommon style of Turkish painting. A similar series decorates the *Jamasp Nameh* by Musa 'Abdi in the British Museum (Add. 24952; two of the ten miniatures are reproduced by Stchoukine, I, 1966, pl. IX). The date 1527 for the British Museum manuscript seems somewhat early for this one, although the catalogue of the Sotheby's auction (July 1, 1969) at which this manuscript was acquired listed it as "Turkish, c. 1530." Meredith-Owens and B. W. Robinson, of the Victoria and Albert Museum, feel that such a dating is somewhat too early. The subjects are:

fol. 67v: The sons of Ali, Hasan and Husayn, mourn as their father is struck down by ibn Muljan.

fol. 77r: The poisoning of Hasan, son of Ali.

fol. 100v: The young martyrs hold up their heads after decapitation at the hands of Ubaydullah ibn Ziyad, military governor of Kufa in 680.

fol. 145r: Devotion paid to the horse of the martyr Husayn, son of Ali, upon its return to camp. (This identification comes from the text rather than from the inscription above the miniature, which mentions the miracle of the horse Zayn al-Abidin.)

Although the style of the miniatures is loose and coarse, the early date of the book enhances their importance. The poet Fuzuli is said to have died in 1555.

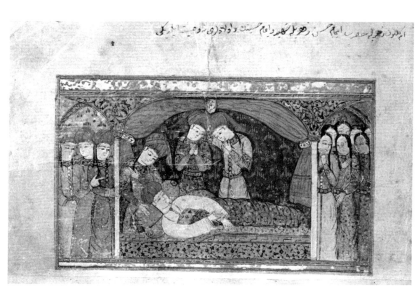

ol. 145r

fol. 77r

5

Two dragons entwined on a spray of stylized foliage.

Ca. 1560–1575. Mounted on an album page with panels of calligraphy. Size (whole page): 3⁹⁄₁₆ x 7³⁄₁₆ in.; (drawing only, not including borders): 1⅞ x 4¹⁄₁₆ in. There is the possibility of an effaced attribution at the upper left.

EX COLL.: Kevorkian Foundation, New York.

REPRODUCTIONS FOR COMPARISON:
Sakisian, 1929, pl. XLII, fig. 69 ("Ecole de Hérat, première moitié du xve siècle"); Minorsky, 1958, pl. 31, no. 439, fol. 7; Grube, 1961, pp. 176–209; Grube in *Pantheon*, 1962, pp. 213–226; Grube, *Muslim Miniature Paintings*, 1962, pp. 96–100, nos. 76–78; Meredith-Owens, 1963, pl. XII; Ipşiroğlu, 1964, nos. 36–50, pls. XXIX–XXXVI; Grube, 1969, nos. 53, 54, 58, 59, 66–68, 70, 71.

The placing of a series of pictures showing dragons in vegetation into the mainstream of Turkish painting has been a hazardous one. The Persian artistic traditions, which were studied and known much earlier than the Turkish, did not at first seem to include such works. When the swirling vegetation around these beasts was compared with similar floral motifs in Iznik plates and tiles, the attribution to Turkey became established. The dragon and ki'lin, as well as a kind of fungus used as a symbol of longevity, were all recognized as Chinese themes, and it was felt that they must have become known to Turkish artists through Turkestan. Once the evolution from the Far to the Near East was accepted, all drawings of dragons were automatically labeled Turkish.

Such was the position in the early 1960s when Ernst J. Grube organized the exhibition *Islamic Miniatures. . . . from American Collections* first in Venice, later at Asia House in New York. That exhibition presented together three major dragon drawings, from Cleveland, the Metropolitan, and a private collection, along with similar ornamental drawings from the Pierpont Morgan Library. Shortly before, Grube had published these and related material in the Topkapu albums Hazine 2147, 2153, and 2162 (*Pantheon*, 1962). In that article was published the dragon listed here as Cat. No. 45 (in the section of works previously attributed to Turkey).

More recently, there has been a counterbalancing of the overzealous attribution of all dragons to Turkey. B. W. Robinson, at the time of the traveling exhibition of this author's *Islamic Art* (1966), organized by the Smithsonian Institution, wrote that he felt it too arbitrary to label the dragon in vegetation (no. 60 in that catalogue; Cat. No. 45 here) Turkish.

Grube himself has since presented a somewhat more complex study of the origins of the ubiquitous monsters (1969, pp. 85–109). He now feels that it was the dynasties of Qara- and Aq- Qoyunlu (Black and White Sheep Turkmen) that

first accepted these Chinese motifs after their initial appearance in Iran in the fourteenth century. They appeared in Turkish art, therefore, only after their prior espousal by Persian artists. This excellent exposition readily accounts for two very different styles. First, there is a group of placid beasts with soft, indeterminate contours, such as Cat. No. 45. These appear to be the earlier, Iranian group. The second style—the Turkish—often features a strong black line, normally serving as the backbone for the dragon. These beasts are true monsters: "alive with almost electrical force," one of which "gambols through wind-whipped 'clouds' of curving branches" (Welch, 1972, pp. 291, 293). It is to this definitely Turkish style that the present drawing belongs. The strongest black arc serves not as a backbone for the beasts but as a fastening for the foliage on which they festoon themselves. The texturing and veining of the leaves place it very close to similar decoration of the blue and white tiles of the Sünnet Odasi (Circumcision Room) in the Topkapu Palace.

The most recent presentation of this style of dragon along with related drawings showing either foliage alone or humans and peris as major figures, appears in the second volume of Ivan Stchoukine's magnificent *La Peinture turque* (1971). Stchoukine places them in the second quarter of the seventeenth century. It is true that the Sünnet Odasi was not built until the reign of Ibrahim I (1640–1648). Stchoukine does not accept the thesis of Kurt Erdmann (1959, pp. 144–153) that earlier tiles were used to decorate this building. It appears that re-use of earlier tiles was common practice and that those ceramic panels and the drawings of dragons that relate to them should definitely remain, as heretofore, dated to the third quarter of the sixteenth century rather than to the 1640s. The opinion of Professor Walter Denny is that the present drawing and others like it were foundation works for the mature Turkish style and that they influenced the style of the decoration on the tiles.

**Two portraits after European prototypes:
a) Francis I, King of France, after Clouet;
b) Charles V, Holy Roman Emperor,
after Cranach (?).**

Attributed to Haydar Reis. called Nigari (1494–
1574), ca. 1560. Mounted on album leaves. Sizes:
a) 5³⁄₁₆ x 3⅛ in.; b) 5⁵⁄₁₆ x 3¹⁄₁₆ in.; (album
leaves) 8⅞ x 5 in. Inscriptions: a) *They came at
the demand of Sultan Selim to Haydar thy
Servant;* b) *One was a Spaniard; one was a
Frenchman.*

EX COLL.: Imperial Library, Istanbul (the so-
called Bellini album, which originally contained
a portrait of Mehmet II said to be by Gentile
Bellini); F. R. Martin; Kirkor Minassian.

REFERENCES: Martin, 1912, I, p. 93; II, pl. 227,
left and right sides; Meredith-Owens, 1963,
p. 20; Ünver, 1946.

EXHIBITIONS: New York, The Metropolitan
Museum of Art, in conjunction with *Art
Treasures of Turkey*, 1968.

Martin, reproducing these two portraits from his own collection, listed them as "Copy after Clouet (or after Cranach [?])
by Haidar Bey, Court painter of Suleiman the Great A. D.
1520–1566." In the corresponding text (1912, I, p. 93) he
stated that he obtained them from the Imperial Library in
Constantinople. It is probable that they were originally
copied from prints of the European rulers that arrived in
Istanbul with some diplomatic embassy. The cross-hatching
on 6b strongly supports this supposition; it appears to have
been copied directly from a print.

The Haydar Bey listed by Martin is probably Haydar Reis,
called Nigari, who is discussed at length by Meredith-Owens
(1963, p. 20) and Stchoukine (I, 1966, p. 30). The former lists
other royal portraits by Nigari and mentions that these two
works were "by his own hand or by a pupil."

دمتكمه گلدی یلدر سلطان سلیمه
مكتوب شریف ایچون
حیدر زبان که

بع اسپانیه دربیری فرانجه

7

Manuscript of the Koran (complete).

In Arabic. 312 ff. (the last 7 are eighteenth-century replacements). The *waqf* of Sultan Selim II (1566–1574), giving the book to the Selimiye mosque in Edirne (Adrianople), serves as colophon. Includes a *shamseh* (introductory roundel) in gold and lapis lazuli, *unwan* (double frontispiece), and 4 completely illuminated double pages. Binding: sixteenth century Turkish leather, rebound in the eighteenth century. Size (binding): 14¼ x 9 x 2⅜ in. Colophon (copied from the lost original onto the last of the eighteenth-century pages rebound into the volume: . . . *the Sultan, Master of the Arabs, Persians, and those of Rum, the Sultan Selim Khan, son of Sultan Sulayman Khan, son of Sultan Selim Khan, may God preserve his dynasty forever and confirm it in the protected city of Edirne, by this authentic waqf made according to the law. . . . Praises be to God. . . .*

EXHIBITIONS: Phoenix, 1969, catalogue insert no. 14B; Bloomington, 1970, cat. no. 2.

REPRODUCTIONS FOR COMPARISON: *Art Treasures of Turkey*, 1966, nos. 175, 176; Arberry, 1967, pls. 60–66; Berlin-Dahlem, *Museum für Islamische Kunst*, 1971, cat. no. 1, pl. 1. (one side only).

The paucity of royal Turkish Korans for comparison makes a positive identification of this manuscript a problem. It is most probably Turkish, this opinion being that of Meredith-Owens, who bases it on the prevalence of blue in the headings and margins and the Turkish predilection for blue and white in manuscript and ceramic decoration during the late sixteenth century.

8

Portrait of Sultan Selim II seated.

Ca. 1566–1575. Mounted on a page from an Istanbul album. Size (within all borders): 7³⁄₁₆ x 2⁹⁄₁₆ in. Inscription: *The Sultan, son of the Sultan, Sultan Selim Khan.*

EXHIBITIONS: New York, The Metropolitan Museum of Art, in conjunction with *Art Treasures of Turkey*, 1968.

REPRODUCTIONS FOR COMPARISON: Edhem and Stchoukine, 1933, pl. 1, figs. 1, 2; Minorsky, 1958, pls. 20–22; Grube, *Muslim Miniature Paintings*, 1962, no. 85; Stchoukine, I, 1966, pls. XL–XLI.

This appears to be from a series of portraits of the sultans, such as Cat. Nos. 19 and 23, but it may also be a portion of a larger miniature later remounted on an album page. Selim II (1566-1574) is known from other pictures to have been portly (see Stchoukine, I, 1966, pls. XXVII, XXX; *Skira*, 1966, p. 194). Certain of his descendants, notably Mustafa II (1695-1703), were truly immense in girth. Generations of harem life and the giving up of personal campaigning sapped the vital forces of many of the later Ottoman rulers. Furthermore, the survival of only the best physical specimens among the princes no longer occurred because the custom of fratricide upon the accession of a new ruler was abandoned.

The rigid iconographic traditions of the portrayal of the sultans permit comparatively easy identification of the various members of the Ottoman royal house. Selim II invariably has a drooping black mustache. His father, Sulayman I, always appears thin and, if he wears a beard, it is white. Osman II (*Gench* Osman—Osman the Young) is consistently portrayed without facial hair (Cat. No. 26).

The style of this portrait relates it to those in the *History of the Siege of Szigeth* (Topkapu Saray, H. 1339). It may come from some historical work by Loqman. It is certainly contemporary with the reign of the sitter, unlike another more elaborate, and posthumous, portrait of the same ruler (Cat. No. 23).

The album leaf on which the portrait is mounted is typical of many in the Istanbul albums. It bears a pencil notation on the verso: "H. 1613," no doubt the number of the Hazine album from which it was originally extracted.

9

**Two miniatures from different texts:
a) A dervish or shaykh on an emaciated
mule; b) Rustam on horseback slaying
a div (Arzhang?) with his sword.**

Probably by the same artist and from the same
album, ca. 1575–1585. Sizes (within all borders):
a) 6⅞ x 3¾ in.; b) 6⅝ x 3¾ in. On the verso
of 9a are ink drawings of three *faranji* heads
and the shape of an *ojak* (fireplace) as well as a
stylized signature.

EXHIBITIONS: Phoenix, 1969, catalogue insert
no. 60A; Bloomington, 1970, cat. no. 110.

The subject of 9b is unmistakably from the *Shah
Nameh*. Less easy to identify, 9a is possibly inspired by a miniature in
a copy of the *Majalis al-Ushshaq* by Husayn Mirza. It is likely
that the same artist painted both pictures for an album. He
may have adapted the probable Persian scene of the prototype of 9a and transposed it into a recognizably Turkish one.
The square-topped flat hat on the second figure from the
right is that of a janissary. The "stovepipe" at the upper left
is the traditional headgear of the Mevlevi dervishes, a Turkish order. The other styles of costume, with their distinctive
brocade patterns, are definitely Turkish. So are the golden
skies, the slightly larger than normal heads, and the general
feeling of "sparseness" in the unfilled backgrounds. The
bright, simple palette relates these miniatures to those in the
Sur Nameh (Topkapu Saray, H. 1344) that commemorated
events of the year 1582. The scenes depicted here are, however, far less complex.

10

Manuscript of the Javahir al-Gharaib Tarjomat Bahr al-Aja'ib (Translation of Rare Jewels) by Jennabi (d. 1590).

In Turkish. 320 ff. of 21 lines to a page, two *unwans* (double frontispieces), three *shamsehs* (introductory roundels), 11 miniatures, and two circles of astrological symbols. By the scribe Mustafa al-Hariri. Dated: 990/1582. Leather binding: unfinished, probably seventeenth century. Size (binding): 11½ x 7½ x 1⅝ in. Inscription on the roundel on fol. 6r: *Made for the Hazine [Treasury] of the Sultan . . . Al-Sultan ibn Sultan and Khaghan ibn Khaghan . . . Sultan Murad Khan ibn Selim Khan ibn Sulayman Khan [Murad III, 1574–1595]*. Inscription on colophon on fol. 320v: *This Javahir al-Gharaib Tarjomat Bahr al-Aja'ib is translated into Turkish by Abu Muhammed al-Sayyid Mustafa ibn Husayn ibn Sayyid Ali al-Burusevi al-Hanafi and was copied by Mustafa al-Hariri.*

EX COLL.: Jean Pozzi, Paris.

EXHIBITIONS: Paris, Musée des Arts Décoratifs, *Splendeur de l'Art Turc*, 1953, cat. no. 625.

This rare text does not appear in the printed catalogues of public collections, not in Rieu, Blochet, nor the catalogue of the Topkapu Palace Museum (Karatay, 1961), and for that reason the *shamseh* page with the title is reproduced (page 42). The historian Jennabi, whose full name is recorded in the colophon, was one of the literary masters of the court of Sultan Murad III. He also wrote in Arabic. The subjects are:

fol. 27v: The Ka'ba at Mecca seen from above (cf. Minorsky, 1958, no. 427, fol. 20). Removed from the volume and exhibited separately.

fol. 70r: Salman the Persian in the grove of date palms near Medina. (Salman met Muhammed, who was on his way to Quba, and offered him dates.)

fol. 193v: The request of Musa (Moses) to see Muhammed's face is granted. First he saw the Prophet and then God.

fol. 195r: The Jew ibn-Saisa, an anchorite, lusts for the sister of the three princes in front of his cell. (The devil tempts the ascetic and suggests that after possessing the girl he should bury her body. Ibn-Saisa prefers to be killed rather than to follow the devil's suggestions, despite a promise from Satan to protect him from her three brothers, who have already been informed of ibn-Saisa's not-yet-committed crime.)

fol. 196v: A miracle of fraternal love. (The single mule owned by two brothers is loaded with a part of the individual share of each brother in turn. As each man makes a trip to his own home, his brother places a part of his own portion onto the pile of the other. This action is repeated by each in turn until, by a miracle, the piles of grain replenish themselves.)

fol. 252r

fol. 217r: Sultan Murad III seated in his library. In front, a group of four dwarfs stand before a *selsebil* (playing fountain). Removed from the volume and exhibited separately; attributed here to Osman *nakkash*. (Overpainting on three of the faces.)

What better method of portraying the royal bibliophile and aesthete Murad III than by presenting him in his library, surrounded by his books, possibly including the present manuscript (given him by the standing courtier in the lower left, who may be the author). The sultan's back is supported by a cushion of Bursa velvet, and he is flanked by two panels with shelves for books of gilded wood similar to that of the Shrine of the relics of the Prophet at the Topkapu. The attribution to the painter Osman *nakkash* is made by comparing similar scenes, with the same large-eyed main figures, in the facsimile edition of the *Hüner Nameh* (1969, pls. 1, 9, the latter with a very similar *selsebil* that has identical dragonheaded spouts.)

fol. 219v: An ignorant old man is told by his jealous neighbors that the sheep he has brought is really a dog. Imagining that he alone believes it to be a sheep, he releases it to get his money back from the seller. He thus loses both money and animal.

fol. 222r: The sultan punishes three robbers, whose finding of a bag of gold has led to a violent quarrel. The first is decapitated; the second, hanged; and the third, after being smeared with bitumen, is released into the desert to die.

fol. 223r: Jesus rebukes three poor men who upon obtaining one bar of gold each, plot to poison each other to obtain all three.

fol. 27v

fol. 70r

fol. 193v

fol. 217r

fol. 223r

fol. 233r: The ant whose blade of grass has just been seized by a frog explains to King Solomon that when God created each animal He provided for its sustenance also.

fol. 252r: Sultan Murad III on horseback surrounded by retainers. Removed from the volume and exhibited separately. (Overpainting in the lower right corner.)

Preceded by five *solaks* (the select bowmen of his bodyguard) and attended by his *silidar* (sword bearer, here carrying arrows) and *chakadar* (garment carrier), the sultan seems completely aloof from the petitioners who hold up their written pleas like candles above and below him. He probably felt more at ease in his library (fol. 217r).

This truly royal volume presents several different styles of miniature painting to match the range of the different tales, similar to those of *The Arabian Nights*. There are two royal portraits, religious pictures, several illustrations to the stories of the compendium, and the marvelous aerial view of the Shrine at Mecca, shown before Sultan Ahmed I added its seventh minaret. While such an architectural plan would never have tempted a Persian painter, it was not an uncommon genre for the Turkish artist. The superb grove of palm trees with the single building suggesting the distant town of Medina (fol. 70r) is equally foreign to Iranian tradition.

11

A prince, or head attendant, in a landscape by a mountain stream. A falconer and a servant bring a slain deer.

Ca. 1585–1590. Size (within borders): 8⅝ x 5¼ in.

REPRODUCTIONS FOR COMPARISON: Stchoukine, I, 1966, pls. LXVI, LXVIII–LXIX and, particularly, LXV; see also examples mentioned in text.

Unlike the *Shah Nameh* manuscript (Cat. No. 17), which reflects a close Turkish paraphrase of the Shiraz style of the mid-sixteenth century, this detached miniature is close to the court style of Qazvin, capital of Persia from 1548 until the reign of Shah Abbas "the Great" (1587–1627). The elements that reinforce the attribution to Turkey are the gold sky, much more common in Turkish pictures than in Persian ones of the same period, and the hat with the curious four dangling ends, worn by the groom in the foreground. This kind of cap is common to the illustrations of the *Hüner Nameh*, a two-volume work in Istanbul by the court historiographer Loqman (Topkapu Saray, H. 1523, 1524). The first volume was finished between 1579 and 1585; the second, in 1588–1589. The leaf closest to this one is fol. 52v in the second volume (illustrated in Stchoukine, I, 1966, pl. LXVIII; *Unesco*, pl XVI), where the large, pumpkin-shaped turbans (*kavuk*) leave no doubt as to the Turkish provenance. The musket sighted by the hunter in the upper left is also uniquely Turkish.

This miniature is probably the left half of a double-page composition, in which a major figure, perhaps a sultan, would appear hunting in the right side. The axis of the largest figure, the direction in which the horse and the bearers of the deer are facing, and the frame-like quality of the mountains in the upper left all support this supposition.

12

Ali, with his sons Hasan and Husayn, visited by Gabriel and a delegation of holy men.

Ca. 1590. Mounted on an album leaf. Size (within borders): 6⅝₁₆ x 8⅝ in. Inscriptions in Arabic: (panels in upper left and right) *There is no God but God; Muhammed is the Prophet of God;* (above the door in the center) *55* [A.D. 674, the year of the event depicted].

EX COLL.: Kevorkian Foundation, New York (Robinson, 1953, cat. no. CCCXXIX).

EXHIBITIONS: Bloomington, 1970, cat. no. 130, illustrated p. 66 (miscatalogued as Mughal).

REPRODUCTIONS FOR COMPARISON: Esin, 1960, pls. 1, 4, 6, 7; see also examples mentioned in the text.

This miniature is probably from a manuscript of the *Siyar-i-Nabi* (*The Progress of the Prophet*) by Zarir ("the Blind"), although its present mounting gives no indication of the text on the verso. The figure in the doorway (his sons have slightly smaller flaming halos) appears veiled to avoid any possibility of iconolatry. The hieratic procession of the holy men, mostly placed in pairs, is interestingly handled by the addition of an extra person, alone, in the second rank. The angel's left wing, turned curiously backward, strengthens the diagonal line of the viewer's eye by insisting on the presence of the group on the right.

The religious subject of the picture relates it to the *Siyar-i-Nabi* illustrations. Of a major copy of that text (dated 1594–1595, containing more than 600 miniatures), only five volumes remain: three are in Istanbul (Topkapu Saray, H. 1221-1223); one is in the Spencer collection of the New York Public Library (Grube, *Muslim Miniature Paintings*, 1962, pp. 102-103, pl. 83); and the last is in the Beatty collection (Minorsky, 1958, no. 419, pls. 17–19; also, Stchoukine, I, 1966, pls. LXXXVI, LXXXVII).

13

The Arabs swearing allegiance to Caliph Ali after the death of Othman.

Leaf from a manuscript of the *Maktel-i Ali Resul* by Lâmi 'i Chelebi. Late sixteenth century. Size (within borders): 6⅞ x 5¼ in. Text: *Let the air resound with your lament,/ Let the angels hear your heartfelt moanings;/ Now hear that which is truth/ As it is clearly written by the historians.*

EX COLL.: Kevorkian Foundation, New York (Robinson, 1953, cat. CCCXLIV).

OTHER LEAVES FROM THE SAME MANUSCRIPT: The death of Ali (Princeton University Art Museum; illustrated in Grube, *Muslim Miniature Paintings*, 1962, no. 81, pp. 102–103); Muhammed preaching in a mosque (The Metropolitan Museum of Art; illustrated in the *Bulletin*, January, 1968, no. 35).

REPRODUCTIONS FOR COMPARISON: Meredith-Owens, 1963, pl. VII; Stchoukine, I, 1966, pls. XC, XCI. See also two leaves from the same manuscript listed above.

Several manuscripts of the *Maktel-i Ali Resul* are known, among them one in the British Museum (Or. 7238; Stchoukine, I, 1966, Ms. 67); another in the Museum of Turkish and Islamic Art in Istanbul dated 1602, with eight miniatures (Stchoukine, Ms. 83). Another text, the *Hadikat al-Su'ada* by Fuzuli (see also Cat. No. 4), is known from manuscripts in the Bibliothèque Nationale (Stchoukine, Ms. 61); two in the British Museum (Or. 12009, Or. 7301; Stchoukine, Mss. 62, 63); another in the Museum of Turkish and Islamic Art (Stchoukine, Ms. 64); and two detached miniatures in the British Museum (1939–12–10–09 and 10; Stchoukine, Mss. 65, 66). All of these have miniatures in the style of this leaf. But, of those of which there are published reproductions, none has a size or text panel similar to that of this leaf. Therefore, this miniature, along with the Princeton and Metropolitan leaves, seems to be all that remains of an otherwise unknown manuscript.

14

Portrait of a young girl standing, holding a rose in her left hand.

Attributed to Vali Jan, late sixteenth century. Drawing with touches of color. Mounted on an album leaf. Size: 6 x 2¾ in.; (album leaf) 12¾ x 7⅞ in.

EX COLL.: F. R. Martin; Sevadjian, Paris; Jean Pozzi, Paris.

REFERENCES: Martin, 1912, I, fig. 19, p. 32, center (dated ca. 1450); Sakisian, 1929, pl. XCII, fig. 165; Sevadjian sale catalogue, Hôtel Drouot Paris, November 23, 1960, pl. I; Pozzi sale catalogue, Palais Galliéra, Paris, December 5, 1970, illustrated on cover.

The very Chinese quality of this drawing has made it a curiosity ever since its first publication by Martin. He saw here a mid-fifteenth-century product of some Timurid artist. Sakisian called it "Persian, late XVIth century" and attributed it to the painter "Véli-Djan," whom he discusses at some length (pp. 125–126). By the time of the Pozzi sale, Stchoukine, in his first volume of *La Peinture turque* (1966), had already written of Vali Jan that he was "a painter originally from Tabriz, who prided himself on being the pupil of a Safavid master named Siyavush Beg the Georgian" and that he was transferred to the imperial ateliers in Constantinople (p. 34). Meredith-Owens also mentions his work, "some being slightly coloured drawings of *huris*, the maidens of the Islamic paradise. A number of these have inscriptions mentioning his name" (1963, p. 20). The faint mark of a seal on the lower hem of the girl's skirt is probably that of a previous Muslim collector.

Similar material exists in the Topkapu Saray, *Emanet Hazinesi*, no. 2836.

15

Portrait of an Uzbek prisoner in a yoke.

Late sixteenth century. Drawing heightened with gold and color. Size: 5 x 2½ in. Inscription: *Bahri Ali Quli* (done for Ali Quli).

EX COLL.: Sevadjian, Paris.

EXHIBITIONS: Smithsonian, 1966–1969, cat. no. 61, illustrated; Bloomington, 1970, cat. no. 61.

REPRODUCTIONS FOR COMPARISON: Martin, 1912, I, p. 5, II, pl. 83; Sakisian, 1929, nos. 97, 98; Grube, *Muslim Miniature Paintings*, 1962, pp. 92–93, no. 71.

The motif of a prisoner whose arm has been immobilized in a yoke to prevent escape is a common one in Persian art as well as Turkish. The model for a picture like this may well have been a captive taken during the campaigns of Shah Ismail, the first Safavid Shah of Persia, against the Uzbeks. It was Ettinghausen at the time of the Smithsonian exhibition (see list at left) who first labeled this Turkish in his introduction to the Turkish section of that catalogue.

The scene drawn on the quiver beside the prisoner shows the capture of an Uzbek by a horseman wearing the typical Safavid baton around which he has wound his turban. On the prisoner's hat is portrayed the combat of a *simurgh* with a lion. It seems obvious that a Safavid-style turban would not be used by a Turkish painter, so he was no doubt copying. Rather than attempt to find an artist named Ali Quli, let us assume that he was the patron for whom an anonymous painter, with a style very close to that of Vali Jan (see Cat. No. 14), produced a masterpiece.

16

Portrait of a young woman in blue.

Late sixteenth century. Size (within borders):
4⅛ x 1⅜ in.

EX COLL.: S. C. Welch.

In addition to tinted drawings, such as those by Vali Jan (Cat. No. 14) or of the Uzbek prisoner (Cat. No. 15), there were others in which the central figure was completely painted and only the background left blank. The woman's cap and long patterned robe with filmy sleeves over the forearms are typical of Turkish female costume at the end of the sixteenth century.

17

Manuscript of the Shah Nameh by Firdousi.

In Turkish, translated from the Persian for Sultan Murad III (1574–1595). 358 ff., 24 lines of text to the page, *unwan* (double frontispiece), and 6 miniatures. End of the sixteenth century. Binding: probably seventeenth century (the text is misbound in several places). Size (binding): 16 x 11 x 2¾ in.

REFERENCES: Meredith-Owens, 1963, p. 21.

EXHIBITIONS: West Coast, 1962–1964, cat. no. 37; New York, The Metropolitan Museum of Art, in conjunction with *Art Treasures of Turkey*, 1968.

The miniatures often have been painted on leaves that bear no relevant text. The subjects may be deduced therefore only from their iconography. The subjects are:

fol. 21r: Gushtasp (?) or Bahram Gur (?) killing a dragon.

fol. 68r: Scene in the early wars between Turan and Iran.

fol. 124r: A chapter heading at the beginning of the *Dastan-i-Siyavush* with plants and tulips; probably somewhat later than the rest of the illustrations.

fol. 172r: Rustam with Owlad, whom he has made king of Mazanderan after the defeat of the divs.

fol. 220r: Human leading the Turanians against the Iranians, beleaguered on Mount Hamavan.

fol. 246r: Rustam unhorses Afrasiyab by lifting him from his saddle by his belt.

fol. 262v: Battle of Iranians and Turanians.

Unlike the more typical Turkish paintings of the earlier manuscript made for Sultan Murad III (Cat. No. 10), this is only a recension of a book that he had ordered translated. It follows the currents of provincial Persian miniatures of a slightly earlier period. Meredith-Owens writes that "the style of the miniatures in this manuscript has been so greatly influenced by the Persian Shirazi style that it is virtually indistinguishable from it. The drawing and the colouring are of the utmost delicacy" (p. 21). Yet there are a few unmistakably Turkish elements here, for example, the typical pointed helmets of ff. 172r and 262v.

The translation of the Persian text seems to be very close to that of the *Shah Nameh* manuscript in Uppsala.

يزدان وبند بوله هم رستم پلتن درد رشته نم قامو سكود وعرولدبخاقانه دوغ ويورويلكرچري داغ دل
شاه ديهيم چون كلب چارون اجار اولور دو برويى رستمك جنله قار خاقانك صوائس ابنك رستمك وكلبكه
حمله قلب انلر قرشو برديب دل دنركنى بوينه صالدكم قلنچله قان صاچردى چرخت
بوينه هيبت صالميشدى كرزله كوكزله بلدى ورنه نوز اولقدكردصوائس يزدلى جقاردى كيمسه يازب
بوربنى كوره بلمكى نقل كيهبقاى جهانك قولاغن المشدى غوغاسى سنانك زخمى توبلبدبكم
اوزنكوزدزكندكل عيان اولكازدى ديبدك ديبدك بوينه كوشنشت كوشنست بوينه نوزبردهصالب بيروت يورتكى آى تعلنلرن
آزردهاولميشدى بيت هواواولدحنزنك يورتكى سياه اولوردن بلكه مزبك مره صوائس بري

fol. 246r

نهيردهدربيان هومان كرك رستم شمدى خاقان ايلهجنك كلب ايلهصوائس برى كوكى برى بربنه اوبرى
ببى اولكسيه اولماسون اولماسون آفرن كه نفرن اين اكا انرگن كبن دبدى رهام دبدى جنكى كلبك بشى كارى

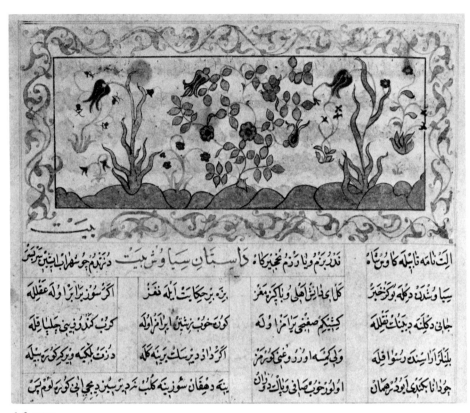

بيت

التنامه نابيله كاوريشاه   داستان سياوش بيت   نذربنم وياردم نمخبركاه   دننم جوسهرابانش برشن

سياوشدی دکله بوکزخبر   کلاحدایثاهلی ویاکترنه مغز   اکوسوزبرابرااوله عقلله

جانی دکله دبیناکتفله   کتیکم صنعی برامزاوله   کرب کنددوفینی جلباقله

بلیلزاراسنه رسوافله   ولیکمسه اوردوعنیکوزمن   درنت بلکیه وبرکرکه بیله

جودانا یکدی ابودرمان   اولورخوبصانی وبالتدنان   ینه دهقان سوزبنه کلب نردبرسبزدبحایکوزه لعمبن

اگر عقل بوسنر زره اوتمی‌دی
که معنیسی قوله اوتمی‌دی
جو معنیسی اکلب بلس
مگر غیبتله نظر قیلس
کر اولو پهلوانکه جهان دوری
دو زگرجه اوله فرق بلکن
قره وسی یوعود اوله پهلوان زبان
سن اکوان اوقیه اوفیل ایش
نه دردس سن اجی جوق شناش
جهاندن ایو ایلو کویش شی
او کوکر زبره زمان ونری
تولین اکبر یوکید بربر کرد
جل رشتم خنجر بله یا قلوبر جز
سا صالح ایده یا فلوری حی
او بو الوب بیل‌کی

دنجی بندیکر شاهت یانی صبری اول ارادن کلب بره شادمان وانیله خندان بروان اولب
کله و تمامه ابر انیکر بجهن قلوب کند و بر بجهن پنه همان رخت آلوب بیلرنی تموب رختیله شاهه کوند
روب بوله دیده کیم بیل لجن نز شیربلت یولن او نردی بره یوب ابواله برهفته تمام عینه مشغول اولب
شراب ایچوب سازند وکوبند بله صحبت قیلدیبلر شراب ازرن رشتم بو داستانی انجوب صبرنجی
اکانت حیکا یایلر کیم بنی شهر بانه بره بربر یاد قلوب که بندخی قولن جهان اجنده اولب و انجلغله

18

Two miniatures from different religious texts: a) Muhammed, his face veiled, harangues his army in a rocky defile; b) The catapulting of Abraham (Ibrahim) into the fire while King Nimrod watches from a window.

Ca. 1660. Sizes (within all borders): a) 6½ x 4⅞ in.; b) 5¼ x 4⅜ in. Many of the figures in 18b have been symbolically defaced by the word *waqf* (pious donation), which has been written across them.

As well as the more lavish manuscripts—for instance, the one from which Cat. No. 12 comes—smaller books portrayed the lives of the holy men of Islam. The text of 18a is probably the *Hadikat al-Su'ada* by Fuzuli (see also Cat. No. 4). That author was noted for his flowery rhetoric, and the short text panels mention the people of Pharaoh and the River Nile, perhaps a reference to the words of the veiled Muhammed. After the Prophet's return from Medina to Mecca, his followers were in almost continual warfare with the other as-yet-non-Islamic tribes of Arabia. It was not until after the Prophet's death in 632 that Muslim armies began the conquests beyond the peninsula that eventually took them as far as southern France and across the Indus River into India.

The iconography of 18b is less readily identifiable, but the miniature probably illustrated a manuscript of the *Siyar-i-Nabi* by Zarir. Its protagonist is the Biblical patriarch Abraham (Ibrahim), who migrated to the land of Canaan with his barren wife Sarai, who was to become the "grandmother of Israel." The episode depicted here is found not in the Bible but rather in the lives of the Muslim saints. For Ibrahim, as the father of Ishmael, ancestor of the Arabs, is revered by Muslims (as are Moses and Jesus) as well as by Jews and Christians. To the Muslim, Islam is simply the culmination of the prophecies by the great prophets of the "People of the Book." Unlike the Christian concept of the divinity of Christ, the godhead of their Prophet was never a Muslim belief. This explains their feeling that Christians are infidels who adore more than a single God. The sparsely decorated interior of a mosque compared with the lavish display of a Catholic church attests to the fundamental difference in dogma.

فرعون آل سيلاب بنيل سپاهى اصحاب نيفيل مغلوب يوب بحو ما
طغرا اول انتدى و توم قلك او ل جار غضند ان كوم لواك

شهرن سركون اميروب بعلات آل نوكك ملكه سيلاب سي

19

Sultan Mehmet III (1595–1603) enthroned, attended by two janissaries.

Ca. 1600. Size (within borders): 6½ x 3½ in. Inscription (panel under central arch): *Tasvir Padishah Zardusht* (Portrait of Emperor Zarathustra).

EX COLL.: Laurent Fierens, Brussels.

EXHIBITIONS: Smithsonian, 1966–1969, cat. no. 62, illustrated; Bloomington, 1970, cat. no. 117.

The misidentification of this miniature by some former owner, who added the inscription about the sitter, is easily corrected by comparing this portrait with others from the known Ottoman portrait tradition (see the facsimile volume of the Vienna *Subhatu'l-Ahbâr* [*Chain of Genealogies*], 1968, pl. 15ꝝ, bottom). The pair of janissaries slyly ogling each other, the pairs of cypress trees on the horizon, and the typical Ottoman architectural detail all clinch a Turkish identification.

20

Manuscript of the Kitab-i-Shah u Geda (The Shah and the Beggar), probably by Yahya Beg (d. 1545).

In Turkish. 63 ff. with 6 miniatures. Ca. 1600. No colophon. Binding: reddish brown morocco with simple medallion design; although the flap is intact the blue and gold paper doublures inside suggest that it is more modern than the text. Size (binding): 7½ x 4¾ x ½ in.

EX COLL.: Jean Pozzi, Paris.

This charming little manuscript opens with a floral *unwan*, above which the page has been cut, no doubt when the work was "removed" from its former owner and some identification of ownership needed to be erased. The miniatures are noteworthy for their simplicity. Most important of the six is the first:

> fol. 7v: The *mi'raj:* the night ascension of Muhammed from the Dome of the Rock in Jerusalem to Heaven. His face is veiled as he sits on Buraq (his steed with a woman's head), and the sky is filled with the winged angels who accompany him on his nocturnal flight. The *mi'raj* is often used as a sort of holy invocation at the beginning of Islamic manuscripts. Although many are known in Persian books, Turkish ones are extremely rare.

The subjects of the other miniatures are:

> fol. 41r: The shah on his throne sees the approach of the beggar.

> fol. 44v: The shah picnicking in a meadow with musicians.

> fol. 5v: The shah and three other men swim in the ocean while the beggar watches their clothes. (The water, normally painted silver—which tarnishes with age—has here been colored in a different manner.)

> fol. 53r: The beggar sees a mounted hunter.

> fol. 56v: The beggar renders homage to the shah on his throne while a servant peeks through a curtained doorway.

fol. 7v

21

An attack upon a fort. Leaf from an unidentified manuscript of the Shah Nameh (?).

Ca. 1600–1610. Mounted on an album leaf. Size: 10¼ x 5⅞ in.; (album leaf) 16⅞ x 11¼ in.

EX COLL.: Kevorkian Foundation, New York.

This leaf and another one showing the attempt of the Persian King Kay Kavus to fly to heaven figured in the second Kevorkian auction (Sotheby's, December 1, 1969, lots 107, 108). They were listed as probably from the same manuscript, and each was labeled "Turkish, early seventeenth century." Several of those who saw the leaves at that time preferred to consider them Persian. Grube catalogued the other leaf, now in the Kraus collection, New York as "probably Shiraz, c. 1600" (1972, no. 149, pp. 168, 171).

The auction listing notwithstanding, it is obvious that the miniatures are not from the same manuscript. The Kraus leaf still bears the full text, while this one has been mounted on an album leaf of definite Turkish style. The besieging army is full of the historical realism that is typically Turkish and foreign to Iranian tradition. A Persian artist would not present the backs of his characters, nor just the tops of their helmets seen above the outside gate. The soldier looking at the flint for the matchlock of his musket is also an excellent example of Ottoman realism.

22

The ascension of King Solomon to heaven, attended by flying angels and demons.

Ca. 1600–1610. Mounted on album leaf. Size: 12¼ x 7¾ in.; (album leaf) 16¼ x 10⅞ in.

EX COLL.: Sherif Sabry Pasha, Cairo.

REFERENCES: Wiet, 1943, no. 18, pl. x.

This is another example of an Ottoman picture following Iranian tradition closely. Islamic literature and scripture have several examples of flights to the heavens, notably that of the legendary Persian King Kay Kavus, from Firdousi's *Shah Nameh,* and that of Muhammed on Buraq—the *mi'raj* (see Cat. No. 20).

The miniature resembles a partially gilded drawing now in the Freer Gallery, Washington, D.C. (Sarre and Martin 1910, I, no. 682, pl. 216).

23

Portrait of Sultan Selim II (1566–1574).

Ca. 1600–1610. Mounted on album leaf. Size (album leaf): 13⅝ x 8⅞ in.

EX COLL.: Kevorkian Foundation, New York (Robinson, 1953, cat. no. CCCXLVII).

OTHER LEAVES FROM THE SAME SERIES: The Metropolitan Museum of Art (Grube, *Muslim Miniature Paintings*, 1962, no. 85; *Bulletin*, January 1968, no. 34); Fogg Art Museum, acc. no. 1958–245; H. P. Kraus (Grube, 1972, color pl. XLVII).

EXHIBITIONS: Bloomington, 1970, cat. no. 118.

Series of portraits of Ottoman sultans became a standard genre of Turkish painting. They may possibly have been used as illustrations of the *Kiyafet al-insaniyeh* (*Costumes* [or *Customs*] *of Mankind*) by Loqman, or of the same author's *Silsileh Nameh*, which records similar genealogies back to the times of the early Biblical prophets. Although the miniatures from this series have unfinished text panels and are mounted on leaves that do not permit the reading of any explanation that may be on the verso, they probably do come from the first of Loqman's two texts mentioned above, or from another series showing the sultans. It is also probable that the portraits of the rulers who reigned close to the time of the completion of the work are actual likenesses, whereas the portraits of the earlier sultans were no doubt made up by the artist, following general iconographic traditions (see also Cat. Nos. 8, 19).

24

The murder of Iraj by his brothers Tur and Sam, and one page of text. Leaves from a manuscript of the Shah Nameh.

In Persian. Ca. 1600–1620. Size (within borders, but to white and purple hillocks on left side): 8¼ x 7¼ in.

This is another example of a Turkish miniature that is almost indistinguishable from a Persian one. The *Shah Nameh* was almost as popular among the literati in the Ottoman Empire as in Iran. In one of the early episodes of his epic, Firdousi tells of Iraj, who was murdered by his brothers who then divided his inheritance. The elder brother, Tur, was the supposed ancestor of the Turks.

25

The army of Shah Ramin attacking the "Iron Fortress," double-page illustration from a manuscript of The Tale of Shah Ramin and Mah-parvin, a Persian romance.

In Turkish. Ca. 1620. Size (overall, within all borders): 14⅜ x 12½ in.

REPRODUCTIONS FOR COMPARISON (historical miniatures): Esin, 1960, pl. 9; *Unesco*, 1961 pls. XVIII-XIX; Meredith-Owens, 1963, pls. IV, XVI, XVII; Stchoukine, I, 1966, pls. XX-XXI, XXVIII-XXIX, XXXVI-XXXVII, LXXVIII-LXXIX.

The great Turkish illustrations for the historical works that glorify the campaigns of the sultans and their victorious generals are of utmost rarity. Few of these manuscripts have been cut up and dispersed; most remain intact in Istanbul. The row upon row of attendant servants or military personnel stretching as far as the eye can see are common in the major manuscripts preserved in Istanbul but are scarce elsewhere. Here, an anonymous artist has used several of the traditions of the double-page miniatures for the historical works to illustrate a similar event taking place in a romance (a similar example is the *Tale of Ferrukhruz* in the British Museum [Or. 3298]). Because of the large number of participants it was necessary to allow two adjoining pages in order to include the whole of the action of an episode. The placidity of the architectural complex on the left, a good example of Turkish interest in that field (compare Cat. No. 10, fol. 27v), is a perfect foil for the turbulence of the army attacking it from the right. The crowned figure of Shah Ramin, with his weapon at rest against his shoulder, and his equestrian companion easily bridge the gap between the halves of the composition. The black dots on many of the faces are a typical conceit from the romances: they are "moles of beauty."

26

Equestrian portrait of Sultan Osman II (1618–1622).

Ca. 1620. Size (within all borders): 5⅞ x 3⅜ in. Inscription: *Rakim Hazrat-i-naq[qash]* (Work of His Excellency the pain[ter]).

The caparison of the horse in this portrait is identical with that in another likeness of *Gench* Osman from the Topkapu Saray (*Art Treasures of Turkey*, 1966, no. 197a). The beardless features have been noted above (Cat. No. 8) as being a common iconographic tradition.

Attributions given in the auction sale catalogue (Hôtel Drouot, Paris, April 28, 1972, lot 169), based on the incomplete inscription, to the work of Ahmed Nakshi or Hasan Naqqash, seem tenuous at the present time.

27

Sultan Osman II (1618–1622) with his vizier Davud Pasha in a procession of janissaries and slaves.

Ca. 1620–1622. Size (within all borders): 9¼ x 7⅝ in.

EX COLL.: Jean Pozzi, Paris.

The rarity of miniatures from Turkish historical works in Western collections has already been mentioned (see Cat. No. 25). The text on the verso of this picture contains part of the story of the manuscript from which it was extracted. It does not, however, identify the episode taking place. The inscriptions beside the two horsemen in the upper right identify these figures but seem to be reversed—the beardless sultan bears the label of the vizier; the pasha, that of his overlord. Their history itself dates the work. Osman II in his war against the Poles was besieging the city of Hotin (Chocim in Polish). Enraged by the undisciplined conduct of the janissaries, he threatened to suppress them. He was imprisoned and strangled by order of his brother-in-law, Davud Pasha, the newly appointed grand vizier. Davud was destituted and killed shortly thereafter, in 1623.

This is probably the left half of a double-page miniature. The elongated tongue of some huge gun carriage or siege engine is dragged by the lowest row of slaves, while the middle row helps it with ropes. The enormous wagon would naturally have filled the center section of the right-hand page.

For a similar manuscript concerning the war with Poland, compare the *Shah Nameh of Osman II* by Nadiri (Topkapu Saray, H. 1124; Stchoukine, I, 1966, Ms. 95).

28

Portrait of a seated man, presumed to be the poet Hafiz.

Probably second quarter of the seventeenth century. Size: 5¹¹⁄₁₆ x 3¼ in. Inscription: *This is the late Hafiz of Shiraz. Since he has been portrayed many times, he must have looked exactly like this;* (upside-down on the border) *Samize* (fat).

EX COLL.: Sevadjian, Paris.

EXHIBITIONS: New York, The Metropolitan Museum of Art, in conjunction with *Art Treasures of Turkey*, 1968.

Despite territorial and religious rivalry of the bitterest kind between the Ottomans and the Safavid shahs of Persia, Persian remained the language of the cultivated elite at the court of Istanbul. Several of the sultans themselves wrote elegant verses in Persian, notably Selim I (1512–1520), who wrote *ghazals* under the pen name of Selimi. Despite political rivalry, any Turkish connoisseur would have appreciated having a portrait of one of the greatest poets of Persia for inclusion in his personal album.

The unusually pale colors of this miniature, the volume of the folds in the costume, and the modeling of the face and figure suggest a strong, and possibly very early, European influence. It is closely related to the portrait of Mehmet II by Sinan (illustrated in Skira, 1966, p. 196). It is even closer to a portrait of a kneeling man wearing a Portuguese-style hat (Topkapu Saray, H. 2165, fol. 12). Without discounting the possibility of a very early work, I prefer an attribution to a later period, probably under Murad IV (1623–1640), in which conscious adaptations of previous works were common.

29

Portrait of a standing warrior.

Second quarter of the seventeenth century.
Drawing with some color. Mounted on a leaf
from an Istanbul album. Size: (drawing)
8¹¹⁄₁₆ x 5⁵⁄₁₆ in.; (album leaf): 9⅝ x 5⅜ in.

REPRODUCTIONS FOR COMPARISON:
Coomaraswamy, 1929, no. 10, pl. V.

This drawing from an Iranian prototype is, nonetheless, mounted on an album page that relates it to the Ottoman tradition. A similar drawing, purported to be that of the Emperor Timur, is reproduced in the catalogue of the Goloubew collection in the Boston Museum of Fine Arts, Coomaraswamy, when reproducing that miniature (listed at left) catalogued it as "vers 1400." This kind of drawing technique is, however, closer to that of the portrait of Hafiz (Cat. No. 28).

30

Portrait of a begging dervish in a sheepskin mantle.

Second quarter of the seventeenth century. Size: 8¼ x 5⅜ in. Inscriptions (effaced, on the cloak): *Oh, I am a martyr. . . .*

REFERENCES: Sale catalogue, Hôtel Drouot, Paris, March 5, 1922, lot 151, pl. XVI (as "dessin rehaussé de Transoxianie"); Grube, 1972, pp. 246–247, notes 9, 10.

EXHIBITIONS: West Coast, 1962–1964, cat. no. 35 (as Persian, c. 1560); Smithsonian, 1966–1969, cat. no. 63, illustrated; Bloomington, 1970, cat. no. 115.

The earliest Turkish artists in Turkestan, long before Istanbul became the capital of the Ottomans, were very receptive to Chinese influences. One group of painters continued to use Chinese elements (see particularly the problem of "Turkish" miniatures in the Album of the Conqueror, in the Topkapu Saray, H. 2153). Ettinghausen's identification of this miniature as Turkish is based on its satirical, almost caricatural, quality. Persian artists did not produce this kind of work.

Under Murad IV (1623–1640) there occurred a revival of painting. It is quite possible that work such as this was produced as a kind of take-off on the distinctive demon and nomad pictures in the Album of the Conqueror mentioned above, since comparable material is found in that album.

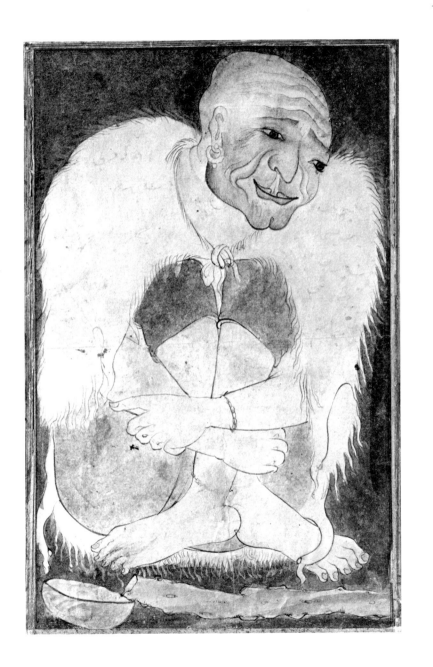

31

Four bostanji (gardeners) in red uniforms beating game with whips, in a landscape. In the rear, a walled city; to the right, palaces and mosques of a larger town. Right half of a double-page illustration.

Ca. 1640–1650. Size (within all borders): 8 x 6⅞ in.

EX COLL.: Jean Pozzi, Paris.

This leaf comes from an unknown manuscript, one that will probably never be identified since a leaf from another text has been glued onto the verso of this one to protect (or strengthen) it.

The subject of the two halves of this miniature would have been a battue of birds. The birds flying above and in the bushes below include a pair of typical black and white "Turkish" magpies. The uniform of the *bostanji*—a gardener-like official—occurs again in Cat. No. 43d. The hands of two, and possibly three, different painters seem recognizable. The depiction of the gnarled tree and smaller bushes is technically very different from that of the typically Turkish city on the right, with its leaded roofs, wooden-beam architecture, and metal grilles. The citadel in the rear was probably added after the completion of the original scene. It shows a perspective much closer to that of a European original than does the architectural complex on the right.

32

A Turkish prince entertained by musicians as he sits on a rug in front of a landscape.

Mid-seventeenth century. Size (within all borders): 5³⁄₁₆ x 2¾ in.

The seeming simplicity of this tiny genre scene is deceptive. The lower portion, with its rug presented as though seen from above, is a typical product of an Islamic artist. The upper half, with its unusual fence of wattles behind a flowing stream, in front of the distant landscape, is much less common. This landscape, strongly influenced by some Flemish or German original, was probably produced by a European-trained painter, possibly a Hungarian, of whom there were several in the imperial studios. The castle in the background, wtih its conical roof in typical Turkish style, suggests Rumeli Hisar on the Bosphorus, or the castle of Yedikkule, near the capital. It might also be the Tower of Galata, across the Golden Horn from Istanbul, as seen from one of the kiosks, or summer palaces, near the "Sweet Waters of Europe."

33

Portrait of a Turkish youth standing under a tree.

Mid-seventeenth century. Size (album leaf): 9½ x 5¹⁵⁄₁₆ in.

EXHIBITIONS: Bloomington, 1970, cat. no. 116.

With the increasing contact with Europeans, Turkish painters found curious their exotic clothing as well as their customs. A very similar album page showing four separate pictures is in the Beatty Library, Dublin (Minorsky, 1958, no. 439, fol. 10b; bottom half illustrated pl. 30b). The youth on the lower right in the Beatty leaf might well have served as a prototype for this one: a similar youth stands under a similar tree, and there is a similar cleft in the mountains in the upper right. But that youth wears a kind of Spanish beret, whereas this one wears a turban. Similar European influence has been noted in the landscape of Cat. No. 32.

34

Costume plates, two miniatures from a series. a) Portrait of an officer of janissaries wearing a high aigrette; b) Portrait of a seated woman, her face hidden by a red veil.

Early eighteenth century. Size (each leaf): 5¾ x 8 in.

EX COLL.: Jean Pozzi, Paris.

REFERENCES (34a only): Pozzi sale catalogue, Hôtel Drouot, Paris, December 2, 1970, lot 151, pl. VI.

The production of *Kiyafet* (costume) books, showing all that was foreign and exotic in Turkish costume, suggests a possible sale to foreigners visiting Turkey and eager to return home with examples of what they had seen. The presence of inscriptions in Latin (upper left: *Dux, sive Colonellus Janizariorum* and *Sponsa Turcica*); Turkish (top: *Chorbagir* [Chorbaji] and *Kollon Kadim* [Gelin Kadin], and German (at bottom) bears out this contention. (All are covered by the mat for exhibition.)

The aigrette of the janissary leader (compare Cat. No. 27) identifies him as an officer of high rank. The amusing "wet-wash" hanging on a line to dry above the head of the seated woman is probably towels from her trousseau, or bridal gifts. Red is the traditional color for Turkish brides; under the veil, her hands and feet have probably been painted with henna.

چوربجی

كلیچی قادین

Chorbagie

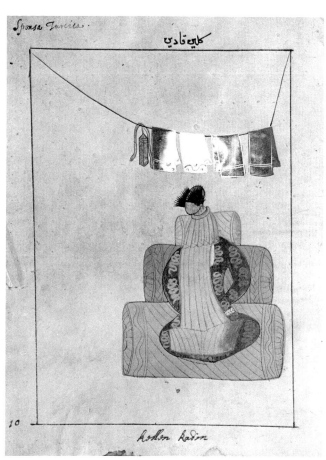

10

koken kadin

35

A couple in amorous embrace.

Signed: Abdullah Bukhari. Dated: 1157/1744.
Mounted on an album leaf of marbled paper.
Size (within borders): 6½ x 4⅜ in.; (album
leaf): 9⅛ x 7 in.

EX COLL.: Jean Pozzi, Paris.

REPRODUCTIONS FOR COMPARISON: Edhem
and Stchoukine, 1933, pl. X, figs. 19, 20 (show
two svelte courtiers by Abdullah Bukhari, com-
ing from an album in the University Library of
Istanbul; other pictures from the album are
dated from 1148/1735 to 1157/1744, the heyday
of the artist); Stchoukine, II, 1971, pls.
LXXXVIII-XCI (from the same album).

Abdullah Bukhari (fl. 1725–1750s) was the second of the two
great Turkish painters of the eighteenth century. Like Levni,
his slightly older contemporary, he mainly painted individual
scenes for the albums of collectors. His specialty, like that of
Levni, was the painting of women. Another of his fortes was
the depiction of flowers, particularly tulips.

After the high tide of Ottoman expansion under Sulayman the Magnificent and Selim II in the mid-sixteenth century, there were fewer warlike sultans and fewer territorial
conquests, the annexation of Cyprus and the second siege of
Vienna in 1683 notwithstanding. The rulers lived indolently
in the Seraglio, devoting themselves to the pursuit of plea-
sure. Many of the descendants of Selim II (1566–1574), surnamed "the Sot" or "the Drunkard," followed their ancestor's
lead or turned to drugs. The most beloved were those who
allowed their more qualified viziers to run the country and
seldom meddled in political affairs. Many of these later sultans were patrons of art and other cultural pursuits. The
reign of Ahmed III (1703–1730), which saw the major production of Levni and the rise of Abdullah Bukhari as court
artists, is commonly called the "Era of Tulips," since courtiers
and wealthy private citizens succumbed to a botanical mania,
nurturing their flowers more than their slaves and paying
huge sums for single rare bulbs.

This cultural domination of the country by "the prisoners
of the harem" saw another vogue—that of erotica. Bedside
manuals were illustrated with scenes showing different positions for sexual intercourse. In European painting, pornographic pictures remain essentially outside the main current
of art, and few well-known artists would have signed such a
picture. In Turkey, on the contrary, one of the best-known
painters did not scorn such subjects. It is amusing to note

that in common with most pornographic pictures from whatever geographical source the lovers do not seem to be experiencing any kind of emotion: their faces remain wooden.

Note: A complete manuscript of the *Ezaf al-iba'id* by Mahmud Jujei Musahib Hazreti Jahandari, dated 1209/1794 with twenty erotic miniatures possibly derived from European originals, is also in the collection. It is not exhibited.

36

Two torlaqs (wild youths) or shamans walking in a mountainous landscape.

Early or mid-eighteenth century. Mounted on an album leaf. Size (miniature): 7⅞ x 5¼ in.; (album leaf): 13½ x 9¼ in. Verso: A panel of Persian calligraphy by Muhammed Amin.

EX COLL.: Jean Pozzi, Paris.

REPRODUCTIONS FOR COMPARISON: Pozzi sale catalogue, Palais Galliéra, Paris, December 5, 1970, lot 94; Grube, 1972, pp. 245–247, no. 225, color pl. XLVIII.

Another example of the Turkish love of caricature, like Cat. No. 30, this leaf presents two mendicants or demonic personages, one of whom carries a club. Their awkward "peasantness" contrasts strongly with the beauty of the color used. The Turkish genius for caricature flourished slightly later in the monstrous characters of the *Karagöz* plays, which presented grotesques as shadow figures. In this miniature, European influence is strong both in the colors and the draping of the costumes.

37

Illuminated firman (royal decree) with ornamental tughra of Sultan Mustafa III (1757–1774).

Size: 48¾ x 19¾ in.

Unlike Cat. No. 3, which shows only the *tughra* of the sultan, this later example includes the text of the *firman* under it. In this particular text, the sultan allows certain French traders to pass through the Dardanelles to reach Istanbul.

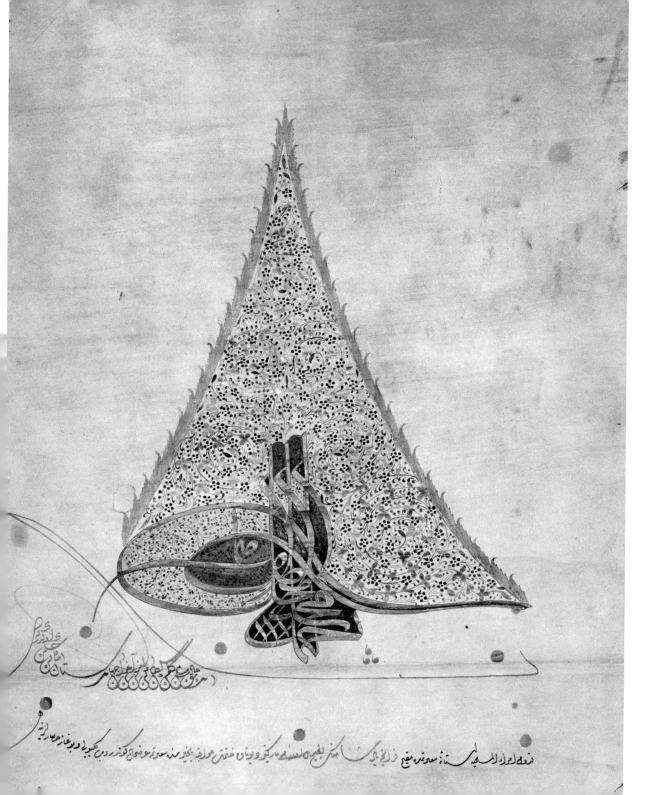

38

Two pictures of Europeans, possibly from a manuscript of the Zenan Nameh (Attributes of Ladies of Many Lands) by Fazil-i-Enderuni (b. 1776–77): a) A woman in a landscape; b) A dandy against a plain background.

Second half of the eighteenth century. Sizes (within all borders): 4¾ x 2⅞ in.; b) 5 x 3 in.

As in Persia, and later in China and Japan, Turkish artists consciously tried to copy European models. With the further opening of the Straits to foreign trade, with more political pressure from an ever larger number of diplomatic visits, and eventually with permanent legations in the capital, the Turks became increasingly aware of Western Europeans: of their dress, customs, and artistic conventions. The best known of the Europeans who settled in Constantinople for long or short periods was Mary Wortley Montagu (1689–1762), wife of the British ambassador, whose letters from the capital (1716–1718) contained interesting asides on the Turks, and particularly on their curiosity about her Western dress (see, *Complete Letters of Lady Mary Wortley Montagu*, Oxford, 1965; Ingres consulted them as background material when he painted his *Bain turc*).

These two European personages, dressed in styles of about a half century later than Lady Mary's sojourn, were portrayed for a Turkish patron, and are considerably better than the many corresponding series of "costume plates" produced for European collectors and curiosity seekers (see Cat. Nos. 34, 43). *Turquerie* was already in vogue in Western Europe; the "Turkish Ceremony" from Molière's *Bourgeois Gentilhomme* (1670) is one of its many manifestations.

Despite the "Westernizing eye" of the collector for whose library this text was illustrated (the heading beneath the feet of the foppishly dressed man reads *Istanbul, city of cities*), his Islamic prejudice against the woman's unveiled face is clear. The calligraphy above her lavishly embellished hat comments on the probable looseness of her morals and comments that "her belly is a place for Muslims to throw their offal."

39

Inscription in tughra form.

Late eighteenth or early nineteenth century. Mounted on a wooden panel. Size (within borders): 7⅜ x 12¼ in.; (of panel) 14⅝ x 10⅛ in.

In later Turkish calligraphy, the lavish *tughras* of earlier reigns (Cat. Nos. 3, 37) become rarer. Courtiers, however, used their form mounted on wood panels as decoration with possible talismanic value. The very intricate flourish, otherwise indecipherable, seems to include the word *Padishah* (Emperor).

A similar panel is in a collection in Cambridge, Massachusetts.

40

Manuscript of the Futuh al-Haramayn (Two Holy Places), misbound with part of the Koran.

133 ff., including 2 miniatures, *unwans* (double frontispieces), and other illuminated pages. Dated: 1288/1813. Binding: nineteenth century, with flap. Size (binding): 9 x 5½ x ½ in.

EXHIBITIONS: New York, The Metropolitan Museum of Art, in conjunction with *Art Treasures of Turkey*, 1968.

REPRODUCTIONS FOR COMPARISON: Minorsky, 1958, no. 460, pl. 39, top (the *Dala'il al-Khayrat*); Esin, 1963 (for modern photographs of the shrines).

The *Futuh al-Haramayn*, like the *Dala'il al-Khayrat* by Muhammed ibn Sulayman al-Jazuli, of which several manuscripts exist in the Beatty Library, Dublin, is a book of prayers and litanies and features a guide to the holiest shrines of Islam: the Ka'ba at Mecca and the Tomb of the Prophet at Medina. These shrines are the subject of the miniatures (fols. 80v, 81r). Also to be found in this miscellany are roundels of calligraphy with the names of the caliphs Ali (*May God honor his face*) and Othman (*May God be satisfied with him*) (fols. 77r, 76v), among others, as well as a calligraphic *Hand of Fatima*, daughter of the Prophet Muhammed (fol. 81v).

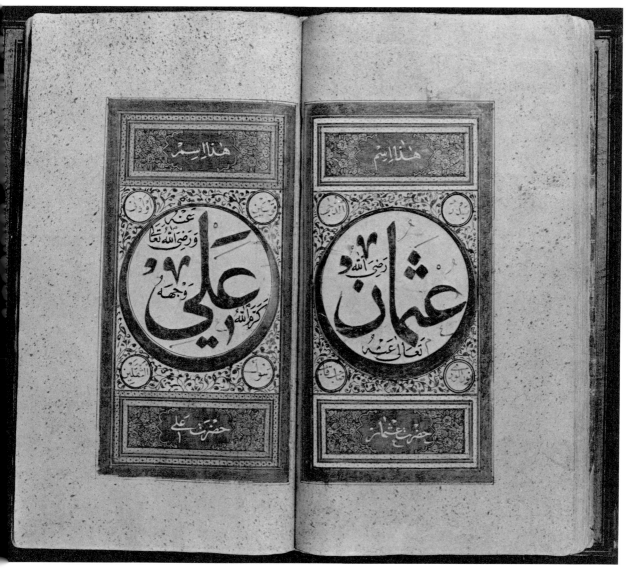

fol. 81r

fol. 80v

Manuscript of the Koran (complete).

Early nineteenth century. On a long paper scroll.
Size: 2 in. x 19 ft. 6 in.

This curious calligraphic product was no doubt used by a traveler who could not carry a more conventional but bulky codex manuscript with him. Its interest is entirely one of curiosity rather than aesthetic merit.

Floral design of a ewer with a long spout (ibrik).

Ca. 1815–1825. Size (within all borders): 14 x 9⅛ in. Inscription (in cartouche at base): *Mashallah* (God's will be done).

The decorative quality of this design recalls the continuous interest in Islam in beautiful calligraphy. The body of the ewer is formed by two renderings of the letter *waw* interlocked as a mirror image. This is a favorite conceit of Turkish calligraphers. Despite this recognizable calligraphy, the decoration seems entirely floral. The sobriety of the plain black and gold against the light paper is very pleasing.

43

Turkish personages and costumes, four leaves from a series.

Identifying inscriptions in English: a) *Kislar Aya* [Kizlar Aghasi] *Chief Eunuch*; b) *Sultan Mahmoud* [Mahmud II, 1808–1839]; c) *Goojez Bashi* [Jüjebashi] *Chief of the Dwarfs*; d) *Bostangi* [Bostanji] *properly a Gardner of the Grand Signior but now one of his Guards.* Ca. 1820–1825. Mounted on a coarse colored paper. Size (of each): about 10¾ x 6½ in.

EX COLL.: J. W. Williamson, 1831 (listed as "Italian school, c. 1820").

European interest in the faraway and the exotic began in the eighteenth century and continued throughout the nineteenth. The Englishman who either painted these leaves himself or commissioned them from some itinerant Turkish artist was interested in what was "unusual" in the Ottoman Empire, not what was everyday. The "wing" on the hat of the gardener and his distinctive red uniform made it possible to identify the beaters of Cat. No. 31, who wear the same costume.

44

Portrait of Sultan Ahmed I (1603–1617), above a view of the Hippodrome and the "Blue Mosque" in Istanbul.

Late nineteenth century. Size (oval): 13 x 10 in.; (whole leaf) 21½ x 16 in.

EX COLL.: Jean Pozzi, Paris.

Series of portraits of the sultans were still being produced in the late 1800s (compare Cat. Nos. 8, 19, 23). Here, European influence is so strong that the only Turkish conventions are the pose of the sitter, his clothes, and the heraldic emblem of star and crescent above him. The leaved wreath around the oval frame and the double fretwork in the border suggest French Consulat and Premier Empire decorative motifs, adapted by some minor, provincial practitioner of Second Empire design.

The scene below is an allegorical representation of the events of Sultan Ahmed's reign. It presents the At-Meidan, site of the old Byzantine Hippodrome. On the railing in the front are shown the keys to the Ka'ba, since Ahmed was the guardian of Mecca. (It was Ahmed who adorned the holiest shrine of Islam with an additional minaret, and this helps us to date such miniatures as Cat. Nos. 10, fol. 27v, and 49, fol. 18v). The turban of the Mevlevi dervishes, a favorite order during Ahmed's reign, is also shown. In his capital, the sultan was the founder of the mosque that bears his name, but is generally called the "Blue Mosque" because of the color of its tiles (in the left background). The space in front of the mosque, with the Egyptian obelisk and pillars to the right (as well as the serpentine bronze column from Delhi, first depicted in this location in a map of 1537), is the site of the old Byzantine Hippodrome. Here the celebrations to commemorate the circumcision of the son of Sultan Murad III took place in 1582.

In paintings like this portrait, the Europeanization of Turkish painting is nearly complete.

Related Works

NOTE: The following items are not included in the previous chronological numbering. At some time each has been called "Turkish" but most of them may come from other sources. Therefore, it has seemed wise to relegate them to "Related Works" rather than to incur the criticism of scholars who might negate the value of the catalogue because of the inclusion of works that may be proven, or have been stated, to be non-Turkish.

45

Dragon in vegetation.

Signed: Darvish. Probably from Tabriz, early Turkman style, second half of the fifteenth century. Drawing, mounted on an album page with designs of animals and plants in two colors of gold. Size (drawing): 5³⁄₁₆ x 4¼ in.; (album leaf) 16 x 10¾ in.

EX COLL.: Dikran Khan Kelekian.

REFERENCES: Riefstahl, 1933, cat. no. 13; Grube, *Pantheon*, fig. 7, p. 217.

EXHIBITIONS: New York, *Persian and Indian Miniature Paintings Forming the Private Collection of Dikran Khan Kelekian*, 1933–1934, cat. no. 13; Chicago, Arts Club, *The Miniature in Persian Art*, 1963, cat. no. 75; San Diego, Seattle, Pasadena, Eugene, in conjunction with West Coast, 1962–1964, cat. insert. no. 37A; Smithsonian, 1966–1969, cat. no. 60, illustrated on cover; Bloomington, 1970, cat. no. 109.

REPRODUCTIONS FOR COMPARISON: Ipşiroğlu, 1964, no. 45, right side; See also those listed under Cat. No. 5.

The whole problem of the dating and attributing of such "Turkish dragons" has been exhaustively treated under Cat. No. 5, where there are references to this miniature.

46

Two leaves from a manuscript of the Shah Nameh: a) Bihzan brings back the head of Human, whom he has slain in single combat; b) The final Joust of the Rukhs: Gudarz slays Piran.

Manuscript in Persian. Miniatures, if Persian, of the late fifteenth century; if Turkish, of unknown date. Sizes: a) 13⅝ x 9⅝ in.; b) 13⅜ x 9¾ in.

REFERENCES (46b only): *Connaissance des Arts,* November 1968, no. 201, p. 129.

EXHIBITIONS: Phoenix, 1969, cat. insert. nos. 61A, B; Bloomington, 1970, cat. nos. 114A, B.

OTHER LEAVES FROM THE SAME MANUSCRIPT: Alessandro Bruschettini, Genoa; Edmund de Unger and Howard Hodgkin, London; H. P. Kraus, New York; a Paris dealer.

REPRODUCTIONS FOR COMPARISON: Martin, 1912, II, pl. 65; Sakisian, 1929, pl. XXIX, fig. 42; Edhem and Stchoukine, 1933, pl. XVI, fig. 32; Cott, 1935–1936, pl. 36, fig. 6; Grube, *Muslim Miniature Paintings,* 1962, no. 82, pp. 103–105; sale catalogue, Pozzi collection, Palais Galliéra, Paris, December 5, 1970, lots 84, 85, 88, 89; Grube, 1972, nos. 66–68.

The manuscript from which these miniatures come was in Istanbul about 1918–1920; according to a Paris dealer, who saw it then, it contained "about eighteen miniatures." At present, leaves from it are in the collections listed at the left.

It was Edhem and Stchoukine in 1933 (pl. XVI, fig. 32, Ms. XLV), cataloguing another *Shah Nameh* in the University Library of Istanbul, who mentioned "des têtes démesurées." They also cited Sakisian, who had reproduced a miniature with similar large heads of the "Mongol school, end of the XVth century" (pl. XXIX, fig. 42) from still another *Shah Nameh* in the Evkaf Museum (now Museum of Turkish and Islamic Art). This third manuscript had an *ex libris* with the name of Sultan Mirza Ali (which also figured in the colophon of the University Library manuscript)—whom Sakisian confounded with the brother of Shah Ismail, first Safavid shah of Persia (1500–1525), who died in 1495 before his brother's accession.

Previous to Sakisian, F. R. Martin in 1912 had reproduced two other miniatures with similar "grosses têtes" (pl. 65). The Swedish scholar listed their source as a *Shah Nameh* written for Sultan Mirza Ali of Gilan, and he dated the pictures about 1490. The miniature on the left in Martin's plate was bought by the Worcester Art Museum in 1935 and was catalogued as "Herat, c. 1420." This attribution merely echoed that of the dealer Demotte, who exhibited the picture in 1934 before selling it to Worcester. Edhem and Stchoukine then compounded these complications by suggesting that the miniatures with the large heads seemed to belong to a later period, in the seventeenth or eighteenth century.

Here the problem rested until Ernst J. Grube exhibited the Worcester miniature in 1961 at the Fondazione Giorgio Cini

in Venice, and later at Asia House, New York. He categorically attributed the picture to Turkish artists, but would not accept the late dating of Edhem and Stchoukine. He preferred a late sixteenth-century date. Since that time, Grube himself has opted for a "provincial school," no doubt that of Gilan, if Sultan Mirza Ali did patronize artists during his reign from 1478 to 1504. Edhem and Stchoukine had mentioned (p. 53, note 1) one of Mirza Ali's descendants who was deposed by Shah Tahmasp and later sought refuge in Constantinople in 1592—possibly accompanied by manuscripts from his ancestor's collection. This could at least explain the provenance of the manuscript at the time when it first became known to Western collectors.

The complications still continue. Stchoukine in volume II (1971) of his *Peinture turque* recatalogues the two *Shah Nameh* manuscripts of Sultan Mirza Ali still in Istanbul (Mss. 57, 58). He again mentions the two different kinds of illustrations to the texts and goes on to explain again the flight of Mahmud, descendant of Mirza Ali of Gilan, to Constantinople in 1592. This hypothesis, according to Stchoukine, "rendrait compréhensible la présence dans un manuscrit de la fin du XVIe siècle [the former Evkaf volume], calligraphié en Iran, de peintures turques, venues s'ajouter au texte dans les ateliers du pâdishah, près d'un demi-siècle après" (p. 62). There is, in the frontispiece of this volume, a Bergama carpet that further confirms Stchoukine's supposition. A

problem arises: is "fin du XVIe siècle" a misprint for "fin du XVe siècle," for how otherwise explain the *ex libris* of Sultan Mirza Ali? And is "un demi-siècle après" a misprint for "un siècle et demi après," since it is awkward to include sixteenth-century miniatures in a catalogue of works dating from 1623 to 1773?

Grube has also restated his previous position, with modifications. In his catalogue of the Kraus collection (1972, nos. 66–68, pp. 102–105, color pl. XVI), he includes three leaves with the "grosses têtes," assigning them to "Persia, late 15th century." In opposition, Meredith-Owens has categorically stated that "they could not have been painted by a Persian" (conversation with the author, October 13, 1972). Obviously no definite attribution can be made until a large number of the miniatures from both the former Evkaf and the University Library *Shah Nameh* manuscripts have been published and compared with those that have been extracted from one or the other of those volumes, including the present two. Perhaps at that time still another category of miniatures, those without the "grosses têtes," of which a group along with others with the larger heads, was recently sold (Sotheby's, July 11, 1972, lots 146–156), will be conclusively attributed. (The present author purchased three of the miniatures showing persons without the large heads. They are not included here, since at no time have they ever been attributed to Turkish ateliers).

برو کشت بیران که ایرا خودیار
من اندر جهان مرک را دارخار
سرانجام مرک ست از نیا بست
بیاده بیود و پسر بر کرفت
سی دید مردان راه و زده و
جو درز د زد شغفته از باه دشت
زپشت اندر آمد براه حلیشی
چوشیر ژیان اندر آمد سر
یزد و بین بولاد خمینه حکبر

به فوجام بر س چنین بیمساد
بین کار درگردون نراه داده ام
بدل بر بدین جای برکرد که
جو نخجیربانان کبرا لبذه رفت
بجست از رستک خنجر دار تیز
زکین بنحم فوبن به بران لبت
برآمد دشش خون زبکر خ دا لان

ازبن پس مراز نده کاینی بو
شبندبستم باج استان ازلنگ
بالا نشاده سراز جای یت
برآمد بازوی پ لارچ
زده بر برسش برسپر برد رژن
روانشش برکشت زان همرقان

بنیذار رفتن کبکاینی بود
که مرجبه باشتی محرم جهان
بیودشر برراه و آسنو

براین گوه ساده زمانی طبید
پسر از کبن وا و رد گا ار بید

47

Entry of the Antichrist into Jerusalem.
Leaf from an unidentified manuscript of
the Lives of the Saints or a Book of
Divination.

Provenance and dating in doubt. Size: 22 x 17 in.

EXHIBITIONS: West Coast, 1962–1964, cat. no.
30; Phoenix, 1969, cat. insert no. 39A; Bloomington, 1970, cat. no. 78.

OTHER LEAVES FROM THE SAME
MANUSCRIPT: Beatty Library, Dublin (Minorsky, 1958, III, no. 395, two miniatures); The
Metropolitan Museum of Art (acc. nos. 35.64.3
and 50.23.1, 2, three miniatures); Worcester Art
Museum (1935, 16); Jean Pozzi (in the museums
at Lyon and/or Geneva); Philip Hofer; Alessandro Bruschettini, Genoa; a private collector,
Geneva. Yet another leaf, Ali astride his mule
Duldul, possibly remains with the thief who
stole it from the Smithsonian traveling exhibition (1966–1969, cat. no. 42, illustrated)
while it was at the Glass Museum, Corning,
New York, August 1969.

REPRODUCTIONS FOR COMPARISON: (from
the *Fal Nameh* of Kalender Pasha) Esin, 1960,
pls. 1, 2; Stchoukine, I, 1966, pls. CVI-CVII; the
latter also illustrated in *Skira*, 1966, p. 203;
(from the same manuscript as this miniature)
Cott, 1935–1936, fig. 14, and Grube, *Muslim
Miniature Paintings*, 1962, no. 61 (the Worcester
leaf); Smithsonian, 1966–1969, no. 42 (Ali on
Duldul); *The Metropolitan Museum of Art
Bulletin*, 1951–1952, p. 109 (Funeral of Fatima);
sale catalogue, Sotheby's, December 12, 1972,
lot 195 (Incident at the tomb of a saint).

The miniatures from this dispersed manuscript are the largest from any known Persian or Turkish work. They closely
parallel the size of the thirty-five in the *Fal Nameh* by Kalender Pasha (Topkapu Saray, H. 1703; Stchoukine, I, 1966, Ms.
89), prepared for Sultan Ahmed I (1603–1617). They have
been attributed mainly to the school of Shiraz, about 1560,
but Ettinghausen, in his introduction to the section of Turkish miniatures for the Smithsonian exhibition catalogue listed
at the left, remarks of the miniature of the Prophet Ali on
Duldul that it is "difficult to state whether a painting is from
Persia in the middle of the 16th century or possibly a later
Turkish paraphrase made at the end of the century or at the
beginning of the next." S. C. Welch feels that these miniatures were painted at Tabriz about 1540 and were prototypes
for the illustrations for the *Fal Nameh* of Kalender Pasha. He
dated his leaf "Tabriz, c. 1560," when it was sold at Sotheby's
(December 12, 1972, lot 195, color pl.).

48

Two leaves from an unidentified manuscript in Persian, possibly a Timur Nameh by Hatifi: a) Two converging armies fight with clubs and lances in a rocky landscape; b) Swordsmen and archers battle before a river.

Late sixteenth or early seventeenth century. Sizes (within borders): a) 6⅜ x 4⅜ in.; b) 6½ x 4½ in. Inscriptions: a) *In the mists of the early morning the Turkish soldiers fight as savagely as though they were Arabs;* b) *After using their weapons, they started to battle with their fists, cutting and tearing at each other, trying to kill. They appear to be such heartless people that despite their beautiful exterior they seem stone-like inside.*

As in a similar battle scene (see Cat. No. 21), the grouping of the armies and the golden sky (in 48a) suggest the possibility of Turkish painters, although the text is in Persian and the miniatures themselves resemble contemporary Iranian workmanship. The catalogue from which they were purchased (Sotheby's, July 11, 1966) nonetheless listed them as Turkish. It is conceivable that they are products of a conscious attempt by Turkish artists to adapt the Tabriz style of the Houghton *Shah Nameh,* made for Shah Tahmasp but already in Istanbul at this time. Meredith-Owens has recently dated them about 1580 and exclaimed: "Dubious if Persian!"

b

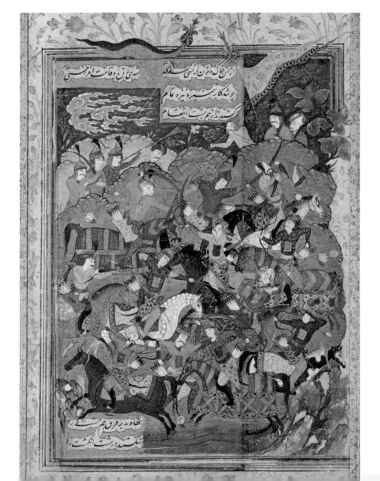

a

49

Anthology of texts in Persian.

The first text has an *unwan* (double frontispiece) and 18 illustrations or diagrams of shrines and mosques. Dating in doubt. Binding (in Arabic): the heading *Timsal i-Mekke v'el Medine* on modern covers. Size (binding): 8⅞ x 6 x ⅝ in. Inscription (on colophon to the first text, fol. 44r): *Written at Mecca the Blessed in 990 [1582] by Mahmud ibn Jan Mahmud of Balkh.*

REPRODUCTIONS FOR COMPARISON: Berlin-Dahlem, 1971, no. 17, pl. 22.

Despite its known Persian provenance, this manuscript is included because its miniatures are typical of a very common kind of Turkish text. Like the *Futuh al-Haramayn* (Cat. No. 40) and the *Dala'il al-Khayrat*, it is a compilation for the pilgrim to the holy places of Arabia. The first miniature (fol. 18v) shows an aerial view of the Ka'ba at Mecca similar to that of Cat. No. 10, fol. 27v. Both manuscripts bear the same date, but the miniature of Cat. No. 10 is contemporary with its text. This one cannot be, since the Holy Shrine shows the seventh minaret added during the reign of Ahmed I (1603–1617). Either the colophon is spurious, or the miniature was added to the volume after the completion of its text. The first possibility seems the more likely, inasmuch as similar pilgrimage guides are usually dated later than the sixteenth century.

Others of the illustrations show details of mosques and other shrines or of their interiors. Fol. 39r shows the Tomb of the Prophet at Medina with the distinctive *minbar* (pulpit) on a blue-tiled ground in the upper right. The Turkish interest in architecture has been noted before (Cat. Nos. 10, 31).

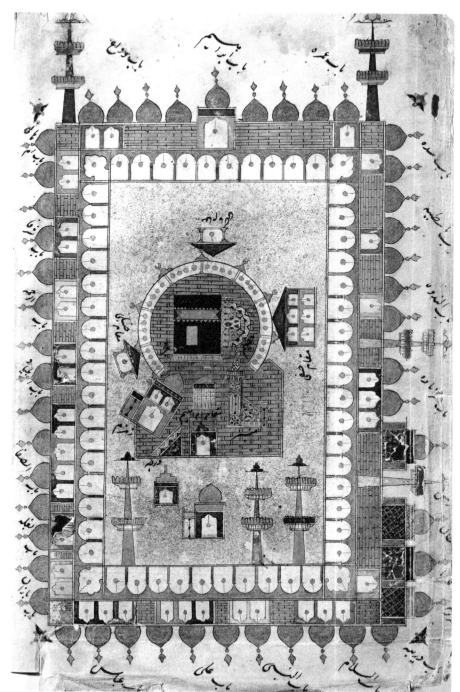

fol. 18v

fol. 39r

50

Bookbinding with flap.

Probably Turkish, sixteenth century. Morocco leather with medallion and corner decoration. Size (each panel): 9 x 5¾ x ⅛ in.

EXHIBITIONS: New York, The Metropolitan Museum of Art, in conjunction with *Art Treasures of Turkey*, 1968.

REPRODUCTIONS FOR COMPARISON: Sarre, *Islamische Bucheinbände*, pl. XVIII.

So few differences exist between the bookbindings of Iran and Turkey that it is impossible categorically to identify all examples. This one, however, seems to be very similar to known Turkish bindings, particularly to the example in Sarre listed to the left, which is definitely labeled Turkish.

51

Kit of a Turkish scribe.

a) Silver penbox and inkwell (*Divit*). Stamped with the *tughra* of Sultan Mustafa III (1757–1774) and decorated with an inlaid garnet. Inscription (under the lid of the inkwell). L. (of penbox) 11½ in. H. (of inkwell): 2¼ in.

b) Lacquer box with compartments for knives, scissors, and other utensils. Eighteenth century. 11⅛ x 3¼ x 3 in.

c) Small steel scissors with openwork upper blades. Seventeenth century. L. 5⅝ in.

d) Large steel scissors, gilded, with tulip-shaped handle. Eighteenth century. L. 9¼ in.

e) Mother-of-pearl plaque for sharpening pens. Inscription: *Jami ash-Sherif*, and carved with the representation of a mosque. Nineteenth century (?). L. 5¼ in.

f) Knife with handle of walrus-tusk ivory. Blade stamped with the *damga* (stamp) of the Director of the Mint. Eighteenth–nineteenth century. L. 7⅞ in.

g) Knife with black handle. The end cut off for scraping. Eighteenth–nineteenth century. L. 7⅝ in.

h) Knife with black and white handle. Blade similarly stamped to 51f. Eighteenth–nineteenth century. L. 6⅝ in.

EXHIBITIONS: Phoenix, 1969, cat. insert no. 3C; Bloomington, 1970, cat. no. 32.

REPRODUCTIONS FOR COMPARISON: Arseven, *Les Arts décoratifs turcs*, fig. 532.

The equipment of the Turkish scribe was very similar to that of his Persian counterpart. Only the *tughra* (see Cat. Nos. 3, 37) of Mustafa III and the tulip-shaped handle of the large pair of scissors proclaim this kit Turkish.

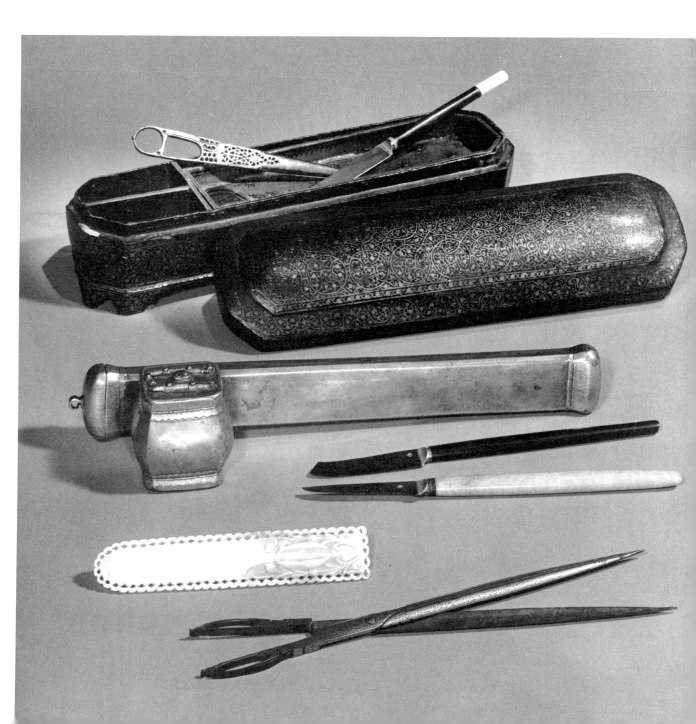

Bibliography

Ekrem Akurgal, Cyril Mango, and Richard Ettinghausen, *Treasures of Turkey*, Geneva, 1966. Abbreviated as: *Skira*.

Arthur J. Arberry, *The Koran Illuminated*, Dublin, 1967.

Celal Esad Arseven, *Les Arts décoratifs turcs*, Istanbul, n.d.

Art Treasures of Turkey, exhibition catalogue, Washington, D.C., 1966.

Oktay Aslanapa, "Türkische Miniaturmalerei am Hofe Mehmet des Eroberes in Istanbul," in *Ars Orientalis*, I (1954), pp. 77–84.

————, *Turkish Art and Architecture*, London, 1971.

————, *Turkish Arts*, Istanbul, 1961.

Nouroullah Berk, *La Peinture turque*, Ankara, 1950.

Berlin-Dahlem catalogue, *Museum für Islamische Kunst*, Berlin, 1971.

Edwin Binney 3rd, Persian and Indian Miniatures from the Collection of, exhibition catalogue, Portland, Oregon, 1962.

Edwin Binney 3rd, Islamic Art from the Collection of, exhibition catalogue, Washington, D.C., 1966.

Kurt Blauensteiner, "Beispiele osmanischer Buchkunst aus der Zeit Sultan Selims II und Sultan Murads III," in *Wiener Beitrage zur Kunst- und Kulturgeschichte Asiens*, X (1936), pp. 34–55.

E. Blochet, *Catalogue des manuscrits turcs*, 2 vols., Paris, 1932–1933.

Alessio Bombaci, "Les Toughras enluminées de la collections de documents turcs des archives d'état de Venise," in *Atti del Secondo Congresso Internazionale di Arte Turca*, Naples, 1965, pp. 41–55.

Kemal Çig, *Türk ve Islam Eserleri Müzesideki Minyatürli Kitaplarin Katalogu*, Istanbul, 1959.

Ananda K. Coomaraswamy, *Les Miniatures orientales de la Collection Goloubew au Museum of Fine Arts de Boston* (Ars Asiatica, XIII), Paris–Brussels, 1929.

Perry E. Cott, "Recent Accessions of Near Eastern Miniature Paintings," in *Worcester Art Museum Annual*, I (1935–1936).

Walter B. Denny, "The Ceramics of the Mosque of Rüstem Pasha and the Environment of Change," (unpublished doctoral dissertation, Harvard University, 1970).

————, "A Sixteenth-Century Architectural Plan of Istanbul," in *Ars Orientalis*, VIII (1970), pp. 49–63.

M. S. Dimand, *A Handbook of Muhammadan Art*, 3rd ed., New York, 1958.

————, "Turkish Art of the Muhammadan Period," in *The Metropolitan Museum of Art Bulletin*, n.s., II (1944).

Fehmi Edhem and Ivan Stchoukine, *Les Manuscrits orientaux illustrés de la Bibliothèque de l'Université de Stamboul* (Mémoires de l'Institut français d'archéologie de Stamboul, I), Paris, 1933.

Kurt Erdmann, "Die Fliesen am Sünnet Odasi des Topkapi Saray in Istanbul," in *Aus der Welt der islamischen Kunst, Festschrift für E. Kühnel*, Berlin, 1959, pp. 144–153.

Emel Esin, *Mecca the Blessed, Madinah the Radiant*, London, 1963.

————, *Turkish Miniature Painting* (Art Treasures of Asia series), Rutland, Vermont–Tokyo, 1960. Reprinted in *Oriental Miniatures, Persian, Indian, Turkish*, Rutland–Tokyo, 1965.

Richard Ettinghausen, "Some Paintings in Four Istanbul Albums," in *Ars Orientalis*, I (1954), pp. 91–103.

A. S. Fulton and Basil Gray, "An Illustrated Turkish Manuscript," in *British Museum Quarterly*, XVI (1951–1952), no. 3, pp. 67–68.

E. J. W. Gibb, *A History of Ottoman Poetry*, London, 1900–1907. Reprinted in 6 vols., London, 1958–1967.

Basil Gray, "Unpublished Miniatures from Turkish Manuscripts in the British Museum," in *First Congress of Turkish Arts*, Ankara, 1961, pp. 149–152.

Ernst J. Grube, "Herat, Tabriz, Istanbul—The Development of a Pictorial Style," in *Paintings from Islamic Lands* (Oriental Studies, IV), Oxford, 1969, pp. 85–109.

————, *Islamic Painting from the 11th to the 18th Century in the Collection of Hans P. Kraus*, New York [1972].

————, "Miniatures in Istanbul Libraries, I, II: A Group of Miniatures in the Albums Hazine 2147, 2153, and 2162 in the Top Kapi Saray Collection and Some Related Material," in *Pantheon*, XX (1962), pp. 213–226, 306–313.

————, *Muslim Miniature Paintings from the XIII to XIX Century*, exhibition catalogue, Venice—New York, 1962.

————, "A School of Miniature Painting," in *First Congress of Turkish Arts*, Ankara, 1961, pp. 176–209.

K. Holter, *Persische Miniaturen*, Vienna, 1951.

————, "Les Principaux Manuscrits à peintures de la Bibliothèque nationale de Vienne," Part II, in *Bulletin de la Société française de reproduction de manuscrits à peintures*, Paris, 1937.

Hünernâme Minyatürleri ve Sanatçilari, facsimile volume of miniatures from the *Hüner Nameh*, Istanbul, 1969.

M. S. İpşiroğlu, *Saray-Alben, Diez'sche Klebebände aus den Berlinen Sammlungen*, Wiesbaden, 1964.

Islamic Art across the World [by Theodore Bowie], exhibition catalogue, Bloomington, Indiana, 1970.

Abdulkadin Karahan, Tahsin Yazici, and Ali Milani, *Eight Miniatures Chosen from Shah nameh Manuscripts* (in Turkish), Istanbul, 1971.

F. E. Karatay, *Topkapi Sarayi Müsezi Kütüphanesi Türkçe Jazmalar Katalogu*, Istanbul, 1961.

Ernst Kühnel, "Der türkische Stil in der Miniaturmalerei des XV. und XVI. Jahrhunderts," in *First Congress of Turkish Arts*, Ankara, 1961, pp. 246–250.

————, "Die osmanische Tughra," in *Kunst des Orients*, II (1953), pp. 69–82.

C. J. Lamm, "Miniatures from the Reign of Bayazid II in a Ms belonging to Uppsala University Library," in *Orientalia Suecana*, I (1953), pp. 95–114.

F. R. Martin, *The Miniature Painting and Painters of Persia, India, and Turkey from the 8th to the 18th Century*, 2 vols., London, 1912.

Hannah McAllister, "Tughras of Sulaiman the Magnificent," in *The Metropolitan Museum of Art Bulletin*, o.s., XXXIV (1939), pp. 247–248.

Assadullah Souren Melikian-Chirvani, "Le Roman de Varqe et Golsâh," in *Arts Asiatiques*, XXII (1970).

R. Melul, *Documents for the History of the Miniature* (in Turkish), Istanbul, 1933.

G. M. Meredith-Owens, "A Copy of the Rawzat al-Safa with Turkish Miniatures," in *Paintings from Islamic Lands* (Oriental Studies, IV), Oxford, 1969, pp. 110–123.

————, *Turkish Miniatures*, London, 1963.

The Metropolitan Museum of Art Bulletin, January 1968 (issue devoted to the exhibition *Art Treasures of Turkey*).

The Miniature in Persian Art [by Everett McNear], exhibition catalogue, Chicago, 1963.

V. Minorsky, *The Chester Beatty Library, a Catalogue of*

the Turkish Manuscripts and Miniatures, Dublin, 1958.

Tahsin Öz, 50 Masterpieces, The Topkapi Saray Museum, n.d.

————, "La Miniature turque islamique," in La Turquie moderne, March 1963.

Ralph Pinder-Wilson, "Tughras of Suleyman the Magnificent," in British Museum Quarterly, XXIII (1960), no. 1, pp. 23–25.

David Talbot Rice, Constantinople, Byzantium, Istanbul, London, 1965.

————, Islamic Art, a Survey, New York—Washington, D.C., 1965.

Rudolf Riefstahl, Persian and Indian Miniature Paintings Forming the Private Collection of Dikran Khan Kelekian, exhibition catalogue, New York, 1933.

C. Rieu, Catalogue of the Turkish Manuscripts in the British Museum, London, 1888.

B. W. Robinson, A Descriptive Catalogue of the Persian Paintings in the Bodleian Library, Oxford, 1958.

————, "The Kevorkian Collection, Islamic and Indian Illustrated Manuscripts, Miniature Paintings, and Drawings," (unpublished catalogue, New York, 1953).

Arménag Beg Sakisian, La Miniature persane du XIIe au XVIIe siècle, Paris—Brussels, 1929.

————, "La Peinture à Constantinople et Abdullah Boukhari," in Revue de l'Art, ancien et moderne, LIV (1928), pp. 191–201.

————, "Turkish Miniatures," in The Burlington Magazine, LXXXVII (1945), pp. 224–232.

F. Sarre, Islamische Bucheinbände (Buchkunst des Orient, no. 1), Berlin, n.d.

F. Sarre and F. R. Martin, Die Ausstellung von Meisterwerke muhammedanischer Kunst, Munich, 1910.

Skira: see Akurgal et al.

Splendeur de l'art turc, exhibition catalogue, Paris, 1953.

Ivan Stchoukine, La Peinture turque d'après les manuscrits illustrés, Ier Partie, de Sulayman Ier à Osman II (1520–1622), Paris, 1966.

————, La Peinture turque d'après les manuscrits illustrés, IIme Partie, de Murad IV à Mustafa III (1623–1773), Paris, 1971.

Ivan Stchoukine, Barbara Fleming, Paul Luft, and Hanna Sohrweide, Illuminierte islamische Handscriften, Wiesbaden, 1971.

Subhatu'l-Ahbâr (Chain of Genealogies) facsimile volume of the Vienna manuscript, Istanbul, 1968.

Zeki Velidi Togan, On the Miniatures in Istanbul Libraries, Istanbul, 1963.

Türk el Sanatlani (Turkish Handicrafts; also in French and German), Istanbul, n.d.

Turkey, Ancient Miniatures, preface by Richard Ettinghausen, introduction by M. S. Ipşiroğlu and S. Eyubloğlu, New York, 1961. Abbreviated as: Unesco.

Turkish Art: Seljuk and Ottoman Period, exhibition catalogue, London, 1967.

Unesco: see Turkey, Ancient Miniatures.

A. Süheyl Ünver, Levni, Istanbul, 1971.

————, Ressam Levni, Hayatu ve Eserleri, Istanbul, 1949.

————, Ressam Nigâri, Hayatu ve Eserleri, Ankara, 1946.

Welch, Stuart C., "Two Drawings, a Tile, a Dish, and a Pair of Scissors," in Islamic Art in The Metropolitan Museum of Art, New York, 1972, pp. 291–298.

G. Wiet, Miniatures persanes, turques, et indiennes, Collection de son Excellence Sherif Sabry Pacha, Cairo, 1943.

Paul Wittek, "La Toughra ottomane," in Byzantium, no. 18 (1948), no. 20 (1950).

K. Yetkin, L'Ancienne Peinture turque, du XIIe au XVIIIe siècle, Paris, 1970.

List of Exhibitions

Bloomington, Indiana University Art Museum, *Islamic Art across the World*, 1970.

Chicago, Arts Club, *The Miniature in Persian Art*, 1963.

New York, *Persian and Indian Miniature Paintings Forming the Private Collection of Dikran Khan Kelekian*, 1933–1934.

New York, The Metropolitan Museum of Art, *Art Treasures of Turkey*, 1968.

Paris, Musée des Arts Décoratifs, *Splendeur de l'art turc*, 1953.

Paris, Rug Center of Louis de Poortère, *Sur les Traces de Soliman le Magnifique*, n.d.

Phoenix, Arizona, Art Museum, *Islamic Art from the Collection of Edwin Binney 3rd*, 1969. (An exhibition of the works listed under Smithsonian, 1966–1969, with supplemental material.)

Portland, Oregon, Art Museum, *Persian and Indian Miniatures from the Collection of Edwin Binney 3rd*, 1962.

Smithsonian Institution, traveling exhibition, *Art Treasures of Turkey*, 1966.

Smithsonian Institution, traveling exhibition, *Islamic Art from the Collection of Edwin Binney 3rd*, 1966–1969.

Venice, Cini Foundation/New York, Asia House, *Muslim Miniature Paintings from the XIII to XIX Century from Collections in the United States and Canada*, 1962.

West Coast Museums, *Persian and Indian Miniatures from the Collection of Edwin Binney 3rd*, 1962–1964. (An exhibition containing most of the works exhibited under Portland, 1962.)

10460